The Misunderstood Economy

THE MISUNDERSTOOD ECONOMY

What Counts and How to Count It

Robert Eisner

Harvard Business School Press

Boston, Massachusetts

Published by the Harvard Business School Press
in hardcover, 1994; in paperback, 1995

Printed in the United States of America

99 98 97 96 95   5 4 3 2 1 (pbk)

Library of Congress Cataloging-in-Publication Data

Eisner, Robert.
   The misunderstood economy : what counts and how to count it / Robert
Eisner.
       p. cm.
   Includes bibliographical references and index.
   ISBN 0-87584-443-X (alk. paper) (hc)
   ISBN 0-87584-642-4 (pbk)
   1. United States—Economic conditions—1981–
   2. Economics—United States. I. Title.
   HC106.8.E45   1994
   330.973—dc20   93-31481
                                                           CIP

The paper used in this publication meets the requirements of the American
National Standard for Permanence of Paper for Printed Library Materials
Z39.49-1984.

CONTENTS

LIST OF TABLES

LIST OF FIGURES

PREFACE

I am fond of beginning my principles of economics class with illustrations of the logical fallacy of composition, the incorrect deduction that what is true of the part is therefore true of the whole.

There are many ready examples outside economics. If I grade on a strict curve, I point out, so that exactly 15 percent of the class will receive an *A*, students who study harder will have a better chance of getting an *A*. But no matter how hard they all study, they will not raise the total number of *A*s.

Another example for my student audience: if a sellout is expected for a big football game—not a likely occurrence in recent years at Northwestern—arriving at the stadium early offers fans a better chance of getting a seat. But announcements from the university's president urging everyone to get in line early will not get a single additional person in to see the game.

Then, turning to economics, I ask my students, "How many of you think you can manage to have less money at the end of the week than at the beginning?" Some snicker, and virtually all hands go up. They can of course spend their money easily enough, or even lend it. I add, though, that I have an understanding with Alan Greenspan and the authorities at the Federal Reserve that they will, for at least one week, keep the total quantity of money in the economy constant. This is undoubtedly beyond their capacity, but on the assumption that they somehow could pull it off, it becomes clear that when one person gets rid of money, by spending or lending it, someone else acquires it. No matter how hard we all try, we cannot reduce our aggregate holdings of money—or increase them—if some higher power is keeping that quantity fixed.

Another good example that sons and daughters of the nation's heartland still understand relates to agriculture. Each individual farmer can increase his income by working harder and bringing a bigger crop to market. But if all work harder and bring bigger crops to market, the increase in supply may so lower prices that total incomes—hence each individual income—may well be less.

And what about remedies for unemployment? Will advising laid-off executives to prepare better resumes help? Or are the unemployed like the losers in a game of musical chairs in which the fastest children survive but one in each round is inevitably left out?

Will lower wages help? A single firm may find that if it can get its workers to accept sharply lower wages, it can lower prices and sell enough of its product to avoid lay-offs and perhaps increase hiring. Does this mean that all firms should cut wages as a remedy for unemployment? Or will falling wages and prices in general reduce purchasing power and leave all firms no better off—or worse off, if would-be customers hold off buying in anticipation of lower prices in the future?

The role of prices is widely misunderstood. Most of us proclaim ourselves against higher prices and inflation. Of course we hate to *pay* higher prices. But for every buyer there is a seller. We do not like to pay more for a house, but if we are sellers, we are happy to receive higher prices. And we don't mind buying our house at a low price and selling it later at a higher price. If we are producers, we are happy to buy raw materials at low prices and later sell our finished product at higher prices.

We like lower interest rates if we are borrowing to buy consumer durable goods or houses or if we are businesses raising funds for investment in new plant and equipment. Many homeowners have recently increased their cash flow substantially by refinancing mortgages at lower rates. But again, the number of those paying lower rates of interest are matched by those receiving lower rates on savings accounts and certificates of deposit. In fact, they are more than matched. Those collecting interest on government securities are also receiving less, and the only gainer here is the government.

Much popular understanding of the economy is bedeviled by a failure to recognize that the common view is that of the individual and not of the economy as a whole. I shall remind the reader of this with regard to many of the most widely discussed and critical issues of national policy: budget deficits and debt, trade deficits and "debt" to the rest of the world, national saving and investment, inflation and economic growth, and the fundamental measures of economic welfare.

The best business leader may know how to promote the interest of a company in the marketplace. But applying rules good for an individual firm to the economy may prove disastrous. One firm that deems its debt dangerously high may decide to delay investment in new facilities until it can be financed more advantageously. The firm may cut costs and try to maintain prices even with falling sales. But if the national government, in the face of a recession, endeavors to cut spending and raise tax rates to maintain tax revenues so that debt and deficit can be held down, the repercussions to the nation's businesses, and to the economy as a whole, may prove grave. Companies lose their customers—who may be the government itself or members of the public whose purchasing power has been reduced by either the increase in taxes or the cut in government spending. Surprising numbers of politicians, though, seem to push for just such government retrenchment.

One of the few wise adages credited to economists is, "There is no such thing as a free lunch." But for the economy as a whole there may be a free lunch, and failing to take advantage of it may leave some of us without dinner as well. This relates to the useful economic concept of "opportunity cost." The cost of anything is what has to be sacrificed to get it.

What then would be the cost of providing lunch to the needy if we used surplus food that would otherwise be wasted? Would there be a cost to government's giving lunch to hungry children? Would the people, otherwise unemployed, who might be paid to prepare the lunches perhaps thus secure the wherewithal to buy dinner?

The reader is asked to approach the pages that follow with an open, if skeptical, mind. Recalling those who for centuries could not imagine the earth as other than flat, with the stars in the heavens revolving around it, should remind us that matters are not always as they appear. What seems vice for the individual may be virtue for the nation.

Over half a century ago, in the lingering economic crisis of the Great Depression for which the prevailing orthodoxy in the economics profession seemed to have no answer, a book emerged that changed the face of economics. John Maynard Keynes began the preface to his then-revolutionary *General Theory of Employment, Interest and Money* with the remark, "This book is chiefly addressed to my fellow economists. I hope that it will be intelligible to others."

I hope my colleagues will read it, but *this* book is largely addressed to other than professional economists. It is aimed at business executives, financial managers, politicians at every level, and, most important, the considerable body of citizens perplexed and frustrated by strident and confusing arguments as to how to move our nation out of its current economic malaise.

I trust that my professional colleagues will find little in it that they can reject out of hand. We have argued a number of the more controversial points within our esoteric journals for some years, but the debate is still emerging.

It is time for a wider public to have some understanding of the dimensions of that debate and the stakes involved. Economics has the reputation of being "the dismal science." Yet, neither it nor the economy it presumes to elucidate need be dismal. Perhaps this book can help us see our way to a better economy *as a whole* and to a better world, tomorrow and in the years ahead.

I am most grateful to Robert J. Gordon and Allen L. Sinai for comments on much, if not all, of the manuscript. I am similarly grateful for comments and help: regarding Chapter 2, to Carol S. Carson; regarding Chapter 4, to J. Stephen Landefeld; and regarding Chapter 6, to Harry C. Ballantyne, Stephen Goss, Laurence J. Kotlikoff, and Robert J. Myers. Mary Eccles and Edith Eisner contributed useful editorial suggestions.

The work would hardly have been possible without the help of a long line of excellent undergraduate research assistants. Most recent have been Satish Reddy and, through the final frenzied labor of completing the manuscript and its tables and figures, David A. Perry.

And my warm appreciation is due to the Harvard Business School Press: to its director Paula Duffy, and to Scott Mahler, then with the press, for persuading me to undertake this work; to Natalie Greenberg, who has led me to innumerable editorial improvements; to Holly Webber, my diligent, efficient copyeditor; and to Nick Philipson, my editor, who has been of invaluable assistance throughout.

The Misunderstood Economy

CHAPTER 1

What's It All About?

"At every stage in the growth of [the English public] debt it has been seriously asserted by wise men that bankruptcy and ruin were at hand. Yet still the debt went on growing; and still bankruptcy and ruin were as remote as ever."—Lord Thomas Babington Macaulay, on the English public debt originating in the seventeenth century, in *History of England from the Accession of James the Second,* Harper and Brothers, 1862, vol. 4, pp. 410–411.

"A long experience justifies us in believing that England may in the twentieth century, be better able to pay a debt of sixteen hundred millions than she is at the present time to bear her present load. But be this as it may, those who so confidently predicted that she must sink, first under a debt of fifty millions, then under a debt of eighty millions, then under a debt of a hundred and forty millions, and lastly under a debt of eight hundred millions were beyond all doubt under a two-fold mistake. They greatly overrated the pressure of the burden: they greatly underrated the strength by which the burden was to be borne."—Macaulay, pp. 414–415.

"Whether that which increaseth the stock of a nation be not a means of increasing its trade? And whether that which increaseth the current credit of a nation may not be said to increase its stock? Whether the credit of the public funds be not a mine of gold to England? And whether any step that should lessen this credit ought to be dreaded?"—George Bishop Berkeley, on the value of England's public debt, 1735.[1]

---

[1]Quoted in James D. Savage, *Balanced Budgets and American Politics,* (Ithaca and London: Cornell University Press, 1988), p. 54. I am most grateful to Dr. Savage for

There was a telling moment during the 1992 presidential campaign, in the pivotal second debate at Richmond. An earnest woman in the audience asked President Bush how "the debt" affected him personally. For an instant I thought, "What a penetrating question, one that few think to ask, and one not at all easy to answer!" How many Americans *can* answer it?

President Bush looked perplexed. He indicated that he did not understand the question. He was stumped. I knew what *I* would have meant by that question, but I was not sure I knew what the questioner was after. I might have offered my own complicated answer to *my* question—on the one hand and then on the other—in the manner for which economists are famous. But what did the questioner want to know?

The moderator Carole Simpson, with quick insight, came to the rescue. She suggested to the questioner that what she had in mind was how the recession and accompanying hard times affected the president personally, and the questioner nodded appreciatively.

Debt is something that on a personal level we all see as a burden. If we lose our jobs, we may have to borrow to keep food on the table or to pay the rent. Debt and hard times to that questioner were synonymous.

Bill Clinton took the question, now clarified, and ran with it. He explained how closely he had come to know the economic suffering and hardship of people and what it meant to them. He won over the questioner and enough millions of Americans to win the election. "The Economy, Stupid!" had become the watchword of his campaign.

President Clinton's success now depends decisively on his ability to improve the well-being of the American people, and a dominant ingredient of that well-being is the state of the economy. But do all of the millions who voted for him, and the astonishing 20 million who voted for Ross Perot, or, for

---

this excellent work which has been the source of, or led me to, many of the quotations that I have used as heads to this and subsequent chapters.

that matter, those who stuck by George Bush, yet understand that the federal debt is not a measure of economic suffering or even, in any clear way, related to it?

What are appropriate measures of the economy? What can they tell us about the people's suffering or well-being? They are not and cannot be our ill-perceived and mismeasured budget deficits and debt. They are not the amount of government "spending" or taxes. They are not our trade deficits or imbalance between exports and imports or the amount of foreign investment in the United States, which have provoked the misleading and inaccurate charge that we have become "the world's greatest debtor nation."

One clue to the answer may be seen in Gallup Poll results reported just before President Clinton's initial State of the Union address. "Which is more important," respondents were asked, "creating jobs or reducing the deficit?" Despite the repeated warnings of deficit disaster and widespread, if unthinking, endorsement of the proposition that deficits must be reduced, the answers were 65 percent for creating jobs and only 28 percent for reducing the deficit.

The greatest economic disaster that can confront the average American, after all, is unemployment. Our measures of employment and unemployment describe a critical element of the real economy. With jobs we create the sustenance of life. Without them we have nothing—and are nothing.

The great mark of adulthood for many, I suspect, is not their first sexual experience. It is the acquisition of a job that brings economic independence. With a job a boy truly realizes his manhood. And now, with jobs, women can move to full realization of their identities.

But as psychologically significant as employment is in our interdependent society, working is still largely a means to an end. The end is sustenance of life—what our labor produces in the goods and services we all use. It is food and clothing, travel and amusement, books and education, police services and health care, automobiles and television. Generally, the more we have of these the better off we think we are. And we can have more of them if more people are working to produce them or, of course, if those already working become more productive. The examples above constitute in large part what we call current consumption, private or public, or the services that are essential to the production and enjoyment of goods for consumption.

Life is short, but it does last more than a day. Measures of the economy must include not only current consumption but also saving—provision for future consumption. Since today's bread quickly goes stale, to provide for future consumption we must provide for future production. That, in turn, requires well-trained and well-equipped future workers in future jobs. To have more tomorrow we must devote more today to the accumulation of capital, public and private, tangible and intangible, physical and human. That capital accumulation we call investment.

The bottom-line measures of our economy, then, are the total production of goods and services for current consumption and for investment in our future. These constitute our gross domestic product or, perhaps better, our *net national* product, subtracting the amount of product or capital used up in production, and adding the net income we earn from the rest of the world. In principle, if we are producing and earning more, we have more to enjoy now and/or in the future.

Some manipulations are necessary to make our bottom-line measures more meaningful. For one thing, obviously we should adjust for an increase in population, although how to adjust is not all that obvious. In one sense, it is clear that if the same amount of food has to feed more mouths, each individual is worse off. But most of us know that our per capita income will be lower when we have children. We see some value in adding to the population even though it lowers our per capita income.

Additional critical adjustments would reflect the limited nature of market-oriented, official measures of national income and product. Do we want to count the full value of restaurant meals but not those cooked at home? Do we want to count the services of taxis or rental cars but not those of the cars we own? And do we want to count as consumption or investment the services of police and the armed forces even though they add nothing directly to either? More crime and wars call forth more of those services, by our official measures, and paradoxically elevate our national income and product.

And should we not take into account how hard we have to work to earn our income? Is not a country that earns and produces by working a 35-hour week with eight weeks a year of vacation better off than one with the same appropriately adjusted, per capita income working 50 hours a week with only two weeks of vacation? And should we take into account the quality and length of life, air and water, morbidity and mortality?

Some of these considerations we can incorporate formally into our measures. Others we shall have to keep in the back of our minds as we seek to evaluate the economic sources of our current and future well-being.

CHAPTER 2

Measuring Economic Welfare

"That exigencies are to be expected to occur, in the affairs of nations, in which there will be a necessity for borrowing."—Alexander Hamilton, 1790.[1]

"A public debt is a public curse."—James Madison, 1790.[2]

"I wish it were possible to obtain a single amendment to our constitution. . . . I mean an additional article, taking from the federal government the power of borrowing."
—Thomas Jefferson, 1798.[3]

President Clinton has said that deficit reduction is not an end in itself. What *is* the end? It is clearly to help the economy provide a better life for us, if not immediately, in the future. How then can we measure what the economy does to provide that better life?

A colleague, recently deceased after a very long life, used

---

[1]In Jacob E. Cooke, ed., *The Reports of Alexander Hamilton* (New York: Harper Torchbooks, 1964), p. 2. Quoted in James D. Savage, *Balanced Budgets and American Politics* (Ithaca and London: Cornell University Press, 1988), p. 87.

[2]As quoted by Walter Russell Mead, *Los Angeles Times*, January 17, 1993.

[3]From Paul Leicester Ford, ed., *The Works of Thomas Jefferson* (New York, 1887), vol. 8, p. 481. (Date provided by James D. Davidson.) Quoted in Savage, *Balanced Budgets and American Politics*, p. 106. Savage adds by way of explanation of the political lineup: ". . . during the age of Jefferson and Jackson balanced federal budgets symbolized the public's ability and willingness to prevent the 'corruption' threatening republican government and republican virtue. Deficit spending and excessive surpluses were thought to encourage this corruption's development by placing unnecessary revenues at the federal government's disposal, ultimately compromising the nation's constitutional balance of powers while enriching the moneyed aristocracy who financed the deficits and debt" (p. 158).

to assert that his preferred method of ascertaining how well
an economy was doing was to look into people's mouths and,
as with horses, note their teeth. If they were in good shape,
my colleague judged the economy in good shape; it was apparently providing the desirable combination of good nutrition
and dental care indicative of a high standard of living.

In my younger days, I used to report this with a bit of
somewhat arrogant scoffing. Surely we had better, more scientific measures. Later, I began to wonder, noting the discrepancy between rosy Soviet reports of unending economic progress and the empty spaces in the mouths of so many of its
citizens. If I had placed more credence in the dental measure
of economic health, I might have scooped economic forecasters
on the breakdown of the Soviet empire.

Tourists are prone to judge the prosperity of a nation in
terms of how well its stores are stocked and the attractiveness
of window displays, along with, perhaps, the quality of their
hotel accommodations. Both are faulty indicators. The relative luxury available to moneyed foreigners and wealthy domestic travelers or those on business expense accounts may,
after all, tell us little about how most of the population live.
And stores may be best stocked and display windows most
attractive when few have the money or income to buy what
may be the modest output an economy is producing or importing.

OFFICIAL NATIONAL INCOME AND PRODUCT ACCOUNTS

We do, fortunately, have better, more scientific measures. Before we wade into the vital issues facing our economy
and the nation, it may be well to invest just a bit in understanding more than the usual TV commentator, journalist, or
politician seems to understand about our ability to measure
the nation's economic progress. Without such an understanding we can be easy prey to irresponsible and ignorant slogan-
eering about such obvious items as taxes, "spending," inflation, debt, deficits, export of jobs, and the like. Impatient

readers may wish to brush past some of the more formal material of this chapter and move directly to the imperative issues on which I shall focus. But the more studious may well take advantage of this opportunity to pick up some fundamentals that never seem to be reflected in or emerge from the economic talk shows or other popular discussions.

In the United States and almost all nations now, government bureaus keep up a remarkable system of national income and product accounts. Owing much to Nobel laureates Simon Kuznets in America and Richard Stone in England and pioneers at our own Bureau of Economic Analysis (BEA) and elsewhere, this system benefits from the continuing study and analysis of national governments and international experts in national governments and international bodies and in academe. New recommendations for extensions and revisions are now being formulated in the guideline United Nations "System of National Accounts." The national income and product accounts may constitute the greatest advance of the century in economic science.

The NIPAs, as they are known familiarly in the United States, endeavor to account for and measure the total value of output, generally market output, produced by the residents of a country, and the income earned—wages and salaries, rent, interest, and profits—in that production.[4] This total, known as the gross domestic product, or GDP, and its major components are shown in Table 2.1.

By market output we mean goods and services produced for sale. That output is made up of many of the things we live by. It does not include the air we breathe unless someone sells it to us in purified or conditioned form. It does include the food we eat, the clothes we wear, and a vast array of services,

---

[4]The United Nations System of National Accounts, toward which our Bureau of Economic Analysis is committed to move—and budget appropriations permitting, will move—would wisely integrate the NIPAs with balance sheets or capital accounts, flow of funds accounts on financial transactions, and sets of "satellite accounts" in such areas as R&D, the environment, and household production, which would provide still further detail and perspective.

Table 2.1 *National Income and Product Account, 1992*
(billions of dollars)

Compensation of employees	3,582.0	**Personal consumption expenditures**	4,139.9
Proprietors' income*	414.3	Durable goods	497.3
Rental income of persons**	−8.9	Nondurable goods	1,300.9
Corporate profits*	407.2	Services	2,341.6
Net interest	442.0	**Gross private domestic investment**	796.5
National income	4,836.6	Fixed	789.1
Business transfer payments	27.6	Nonresidential	565.5
Indirect business tax and non tax liability	502.8	Residential	223.6
Less: subsidies less surplus of govt. ent.	2.7	Change in business inventories	7.3
Statistical discrepancy	23.6	**Net exports**	−29.6
Net national product	5,387.9	Exports	640.5
Consumption of fixed capital	657.9	Imports	670.1
Gross national product	6,045.8	**Government purchases of goods and services**	1,131.8
Less: Net factor incomes from rest of world	7.3	Federal	448.8
		State and local	683.0
Gross domestic product	6,038.5	**Gross domestic product**	6,038.5

*With inventory valuation and capital consumption adjustments.
**With inventory valuation adjustments.

Source: Survey of Current Business, September 1993, Tables 1.1, 1.9, and 1.14, pp. 7, 9, and 10.

excluding illegal services; it takes in housing, telephones and electricity, restaurants, vacation resorts, hospitals and retirement homes. And it includes all of the production of new plant and machinery and new houses that enables us to consume more goods and services or to have still more investment goods for the future.

We generally value all of this output at market prices, what people pay for it. That has several advantages. First, market prices are observable, so we get a fairly unambiguous measure, free of guesswork. Second, it frees the statistician from the need—or the opportunity—for value judgments. Is much of the product worthless? Are the patent medicines no good? Are the books trash? Is the tobacco killing people? Not for the measurer to say. If people freely buy goods or services, they apparently think them worth the cost. Otherwise they would not purchase them.

Suppose some firms raise prices or prices rise generally with inflation. The nominal or dollar value of the gross domestic product will rise. Its value still is what people pay for it. We do, however, usually want a measure of *real* output, that is, a measure divorced from price changes. This is obtained by calculating what would have been paid for each year's output in the prices of a base year, currently 1987. If our gross domestic product in 1987 dollars rises, the physical volume of the nation's output of goods and services has risen. With population rising at about 1.1 percent per year, GDP would have to rise by that amount for us to stay in the same place. A reasonable measure of changes in economic welfare, subject to a number of qualifications to be discussed below, may then be derived by calculating the changes in GDP per capita. If GDP per capita rises, say, by 2 percent, we can say that on average GDP has risen 2 percent per person. Of course, this measure tells us nothing about the distribution of the nation's output; we cannot assume that the goods and services going to the average person have risen by 2 percent. A few people may have gotten a lot more, while the majority may have had no gain, or even lost.

INCREASING GDP PER CAPITA

We can raise GDP per capita in two ways: by raising product per hour worked or by raising the number of hours worked per person in the population. The former is what we usually think of as labor productivity. It is presumably increased by wise investment in additional, technologically advanced equipment. It can be affected in a major way, perhaps too often ignored, by investment in human capital, including the education and training of workers and management and investment in research and development.

Hours worked per capita may be viewed as the product of two components: hours per worker and workers per person in the population. Both of these measures have over the years generally moved in the opposite direction from labor productivity. Increases in productivity have usually translated into higher real wages per hour and workers have generally chosen to take some of their higher total earnings in shorter hours, longer vacations, and earlier retirement. In recent decades, though, large increases in female participation in the labor force—it rose from 32.7 percent in 1948 to 57.8 percent in 1992, while male participation declined from 86.6 percent to 75.6 percent over the same period—have enabled workers to maintain their family standard of living in the face of declining after-tax real earnings.

Workers also tend to live longer and to enter the labor force later, spending more time in school. These trends have reduced the number of workers per capita. But they have been more than matched in the past several decades by those increasing proportions of women entering the labor force and producing for the market.

There is no sound evidence that productivity per worker-hour in any individual activity has declined, although its rate of growth has slackened markedly in recent decades. Some measures would appear to have shown actual decreases in output per worker-hour in construction, but these are almost certainly spurious. It has been suggested that changing patterns of international trade and specialization have tended to concentrate new jobs in relatively less productive industries, usually identified as those producing services rather than manufactured goods. This suggestion seems to ignore the fact that many service industries—beginning with the services of computers but extending to communications, financial services, and retail trade—have shown, by many measures, major increases in productivity.

It would appear that someone other than current workers has benefited from what increases in productivity there have been—perhaps managers, stockholders, bond dealers, and the like. Much has been absorbed in soaring health care costs, which do reflect, though, at least in part, increased health services. In any event, we have witnessed over these decades a significant decline in the rate of real wages per hour after taxes. Working Americans have maintained their output *per capita* and their standard of living by putting more women to work. Nevertheless, real per capita gross national product was a trifle lower in 1992 than in 1989, as shown in Table 2.2. Small wonder that so many voters soured on the incumbent administration. The confidence in steady improvement, the dream of Americans that their children would live better, seemed to many to be shattering.

NATIONAL INCOME

The national income, which goes beyond labor income, including rent, interest, dividends, and the rest of profits, is directly related to the gross domestic product, as may be seen in Table 2.1. It is in fact the income earned in producing that product, plus the net income from abroad (essentially income earned by Americans on their investments in the rest of the world, minus income earned by foreigners on their investments in the United States). This comes to the income earned by residents of the United States in producing the gross *national* product (GNP).

One person can receive income as another person's handout, either directly or through the intermediary of government

Table 2.2 *Real Gross National Product per Capita and Its Rate of Growth, 1959–1993*

Year	Gross National Product (per capita, 1993 dollars)	Rate of Growth (percent)
1959	13,582	3.7
1960	13,667	0.6
1961	13,810	1.0
1962	14,308	3.6
1963	14,686	2.6
1964	15,303	4.2
1965	15,951	4.2
1966	16,682	4.6
1967	16,937	1.5
1968	17,470	3.1
1969	17,762	1.7
1970	17,560	−1.1
1971	17,846	1.6
1972	18,563	4.0
1973	19,384	4.4
1974	19,114	−1.4
1975	18,726	−2.0
1976	19,489	4.1
1977	20,180	3.5
1978	20,919	3.7
1979	21,277	1.7
1980	20,908	−1.7
1981	20,035	0.6
1982	20,360	−3.2
1983	20,938	2.8
1984	21,995	5.0
1985	22,429	2.0
1986	22,838	1.8
1987	23,308	2.1
1988	24,021	3.1
1989	24,432	1.7
1990	24,497	0.3
1991	24,022	−1.9
1992	24,349	1.4
1993	24,728	1.6

Sources: Economic Report of the President, 1993, Table B-5, p. 355, for population (extrapolated for 1993); *Survey of Current Business,* September 1993, Table 2, p. 50, for GNP in 1987 dollars; and The WEFA Group, *U.S. Long-Term Economic Outlook,* third quarter for 1993, for forecast of 1993 GNP and implicit price deflator to convert to 1993 dollars.

"transfer payments" such as welfare benefits, unemployment insurance, or social security retirement checks. One person's income via a transfer payment, though, is another person's loss—or that of the government or business making the transfer. Similarly, the national income does not include the interest income received by those holding government debt. We do not then have the anomaly of the national income rising as the government debt and interest payments on that debt rise. And the capital gains from buying and selling securities do not add to national income. Capital gains in general, stemming from increases in prices, are not seen as measuring any addition to the quantity or quality of goods and services produced. The *national* income, it must be stressed, can only be earned the old-fashioned way, by producing goods and services.

A CRUCIAL DEFINITION OF "FINAL PRODUCT"

The great sin to shun in all this is "double counting." We don't want to go to the coal companies to determine the value of coal they sell to the steel companies and then count that cost or input in the value of steel produced and in turn count again the value of steel that goes into an automobile or truck. One way to avoid double counting is to include in the gross domestic product only the "final product" of the economy, ignoring all the intermediate products along the way. The national income accounts accomplish this by counting as that final product goods and services that are purchased but not resold during the period of measure. Thus we count the automobile or truck, which includes the coal and steel that went into producing it; we do not count the coal and steel again.

The definition of final product as purchases not resold enables us to include virtually all purchases by consumers in personal consumption expenditures, since consumers generally buy for their own use and not to sell back to business. It also calls for the inclusion of all business and nonprofit institution purchases of new equipment and structures and household purchases of new homes, as well as the *increase* in business inventories (since they represent purchases of inputs by business that are not resold). And it mandates the inclusion of government purchases of goods and services, since government is not generally in the business of selling its product. These include education, at least below the college level, and the maintenance of police forces and the military—the Persian Gulf War expenditures, largely reimbursed by other nations, being a conspicuous exception.

Although this definition of final product—purchases not resold—is neat and clear-cut, it presents some problems. First, while new equipment and structures and houses are not generally resold during the year they are purchased, they produce services year by year and these services are counted in current product each year as the equipment and structures and houses are used up. A newly produced Boeing plane, for example, is counted in final product, as are the transportation services it furnishes—which we may take to be the real final product—during its subsequent use. Thus we are double counting in the sense of including both the actual final product and the previously counted structures and equipment used to produce that product.

Each year we include in gross domestic product both the portion of output reflecting the using up of existing capital that went into that output and the production of new capital goods that will go into future production. We do adjust for this when we look at *net* domestic product, which entails subtracting depreciation or the somewhat more comprehensive "consumption of fixed capital" from the gross total. A major reason for not focusing generally on this net measure is that just how much to allow for depreciation is a perennial problem, which requires us to estimate on the basis of various criteria or of arbitrary rules. The net figure, subtracting depreciation, is surely more relevant for purposes of measuring the contribution to well-being, but it is also less exact.

The other major difference between the gross national product and the income received by those producing it is indirect business taxes—sales, excise and property taxes, and so forth.

Whatever public services to business or individuals they may in a sense pay for—police, fire protection, education, or what have you—they are perceived as subtractions from business receipts (including the gross imputed rent of homeowners[5]) used to pay for these public services and not as components of business, household, or national income.

I shall note shortly some major limitations of the usual income and product accounts. But, adjusted for prices and population as I have indicated, these accounts are indeed a better total measure of the people's welfare than just the appearance of their teeth. And they are a better measure than most of the economic statistics on prices, indices, indicators, debt and balances, and deficits—common, if confusing, elements in the daily outpourings of the media. The series of real (constant dollar) gross national product per capita and its rate of growth, shown in Table 2.2, may offer a reasonable first view of the performance of the U.S. economy.[6]

SOMEONE HAS TO BUY THE NATIONAL PRODUCT!

An enormous advantage of our ability to summarize economic activity in national income and product accounts is their correspondence to broad categories of economic behavior that are susceptible to the influence of economic policy. As I write it is suggested, for example, that gross domestic product in 1994 is likely to run about $6.8 trillion. For it to be at that rate we would have to have purchases of final product attaining that amount. From where would they come? The accounts make clear that they will have to come from consumers (personal consumption expenditures), businesses (gross

---

[5] Note below that our national income accountants view homeowners as landlords, renting to themselves and receiving a gross rent out of which they pay certain costs, including their property taxes. Only what is left after these costs are incurred is counted as "rental income" and hence part of national income.

[6] The gross *domestic* product is the new bottom line in our national accounts, moving us into conformity with most other nations. I prefer the previous bottom line, gross *national* product, which includes net factor incomes from the rest of the world. These, after all, do contribute to (if they are positive, or subtract from, if they are negative) the welfare of residents of the United States.

private domestic investment), government (government purchases of goods and services), or foreigners (net exports, or exports minus imports). There are no alternatives.

Given this accounting framework, can we confidently support the politician who wants to give a tax break to those who would "save" more? If they do consequently save more, that means less consumption. What then will replace the lost purchases of final product that were to bring us to that $6.8 trillion total? More investment, we might say. But what would induce business to make more final purchases of new plant and equipment? Would it be consumers purchasing *less*? Or would it be some other policy such as lowering taxes without tying the tax cut to more saving?

What about cutting government spending? If the federal government buys less of the nation's final output, will someone else—consumers, business, or foreigners—necessarily buy more? Maybe, but are we so sure? Recently I heard John McLaughlin, the raucous host of the McLaughlin Group television show, ask Bob Packwood, a Republican former chairman of the Senate Finance Committee, in a relatively quiet interview, whether the blocked Clinton stimulus package might not be a good idea in view of persistent unemployment in our sluggish economy. Packwood responded promptly with some passion that not more spending but *lower* government spending would create far more jobs; the stimulus package would presumably create none or none "worthwhile." What made Packwood so sure? Can his conviction—and that of millions of others on this score—be fit into an analysis that makes clear that someone has to buy what is being produced if business is to go on producing it? Possibly, but it will turn out to be not so easy.

We will come back to these issues in later chapters.

LIMITATIONS OF THE OFFICIAL ACCOUNTS

The critical definition of final product in the conventional accounts runs into some significant difficulties in its implications for government. Take state expenditures for road maintenance, for example. These outlays, to construction companies and maintenance crews, are by the official definition part of final product—purchases not resold. But is not the final product really the services of the roads, even though these are not generally purchased directly or sold?

Or take police services. Are they final product or are they intermediate product, essential to protecting businesses that produce the final product or to giving consumers a chance to enjoy it? The anomaly may be seen in noting what would happen to our measure of gross domestic product if General Motors were to work out an arrangement with the city of Flint, Michigan, to stop furnishing police protection for its plant in return for an abatement of its property taxes. General Motors would then use what it had paid in these indirect taxes to pay a private protection agency to guard its property. This agency would hire the police released by the city.

Government expenditures for goods and services would then be decreased by the amount of the police salaries. But the cost of producing the automobiles would be unchanged, because payments to the private protection agency would equal the "indirect business taxes" no longer paid. The value of the output of automobiles would be unchanged. Our measure of gross domestic product would be reduced by the amount of the police salaries, which had been the "final product" of government, even though the only change had been in who paid them—now business instead of government. What had been a final product purchased by government, final because it was paid for in taxes rather than sold, now became intermediate, the sale of services by the private protection agency to General Motors, which in turn resold them as part of its automobiles, which *were* final product.

The final-intermediate product issue turns in the opposite direction in the case of media services financed by advertising. The movie we see in a theater or rent from a video store is valued in final product as what we pay for it. But if we watch the same movie on commercial television, its expense turns up as a cost to the sponsor, a payment, say, by General

Motors to ABC television. It is thus "intermediate" in the production and marketing of GM cars, adding nothing to their real value and hence nothing to gross domestic product.

With our conventional official accounts, therefore, gross domestic product goes down as people abandon movie theaters to watch films "for free" on their own TVs. But is their economic well-being really less? Then, if they subsequently abandon free television to subscribe to HBO or Cinemax or rent movies from their local video store, gross domestic product goes up.

Despite the definitions and focus on output for the market, the official accounts actually include a number of "imputations" for the value of output that is not sold in the market. Thus, they add the value of food and fuel produced and consumed on farms. They also include the value of "free" food and lodging provided by employers to employees, particularly domestic workers, and the value of financial services provided to consumers without charge or without charge of full cost, such as free checking services given to depositors in lieu of paying them some or all of the interest earned on their deposits.

Most important, they include the rental values of owner-occupied dwellings. Without this imputation the gross domestic product would go down dramatically as Americans increasingly abandoned the rental market, where the rents they paid were a measure of the housing services in the GDP, to buy new houses or condominiums, where the owners in a sense paid rent to themselves rather than in a market transaction. In effect, the accounts make believe that homeowners are in business. Their business is that of being landlords, who rent to themselves. It is thus that purchases of new houses by these homeowner-businesses are counted as investment, just as is the purchase of a new building by any other business.

Once we admit the need for imputations of some nonmarket production we open up a whole Pandora's Box. There are vast additional amounts of vital services produced by men and, particularly, women in the home, which are not destined for sale in the market. Virtually all of the services of government—whether we like them or not and whether they are paid for by taxes or borrowing—are provided to the public without charge, that is, without market transactions. And we must make many other extensions and revisions of the conventional accounts before we are able to fully measure economic contributions to our well-being, or the effects of debt and deficits on those contributions.[7]

EXTENDED AND REVISED NATIONAL INCOME ACCOUNTS

Consider the old anecdote about the Yuppie who uses some of *his* (note the sexism) high income to hire a housekeeper. He pays *her,* say, $20,000 a year out of his $80,000 salary to keep his luxury apartment in order, to do the marketing and cooking, and generally offer all the comforts he had come to expect from dear old Mom. The Bureau of Economic Analysis, if it included the Yuppie and his housekeeper in its numbers, would find $100,000 of income going into national income. This would correspond to $100,000 of the gross domestic product that they were paid to produce—the $80,000 of advice that the Yuppie gave to clients of his brokerage firm and the $20,000 of housekeeping services produced by the housekeeper.

But suppose that the relationship between the Yuppie and his housekeeper deepens. They fall in love and marry. Our Yuppie now devotes $20,000 a year to meet his wife's personal expenses, which she had previously paid out of her $20,000 salary. What happens to national income and gross domestic product? The BEA will now find the couple earning only $80,000 of national income and contributing only $80,000 to the gross domestic product. While the same services are now being performed—perhaps, with the stimulus of love, more— the national income and product have declined. Activities that entailed "market" transactions are no longer counted because they have become "nonmarket."

---

[7] A number of these extensions are envisaged in the proposed move toward the U.N. System of National Accounts mentioned in note 4.

HOUSEHOLD WORK AND OTHER NONMARKET ACTIVITY

The story, apocryphal and unrealistic as it may be—it ignores tax considerations, for example—illustrates a vitally important point. Our official conventional accounts omit vast amounts of nonmarket output, particularly within the household. My own conservative estimates suggest that including the value of unpaid labor services in the home would have increased our 1992 gross domestic product of $6 trillion by fully one-third. Think of all the activities we are not counting: child care, cooking, laundering, cleaning, marketing, entertaining—not to mention the value of connubial bliss, which would, if paid for in the market, probably be excluded as illegal, or unobserved, underground activity.

What makes the exclusion of nonmarket activities especially bothersome for serious economic analysis is that they are not a constant proportion of the market activities that are included. Over the past 200 years the economy of the United States has changed from one in which the great bulk of economic activity was nonmarket, e.g., making yarn at the old spinning wheel in the parlor, or growing crops on the frontier farm. Clothes are now store-bought and food comes packaged and even precooked. The bulk of production is sold and bought in the market. The growth in the market economy reflected in the official measures of gross domestic product and national income thus exceeds the growth in the entire U.S. economy, market and nonmarket.

If we compare the United States with less developed countries in Asia or Africa or Latin America, we find that their market economies are much smaller than ours but that the proportion of their output produced outside of the market is much greater. The people of India do not buy many TV dinners. They and the people of other less developed countries are indeed impoverished, but many of them at least are not starving, as they would be if their sustenance were limited to what they could purchase with their few hundred dollars per capita income. Thus, focus on the essentially market activities of the official or conventional accounts tends to exaggerate the long-run growth in developed countries and exaggerates the differences in living standards, though great in any event, between less developed and fully developed economies.

Omission of nonmarket activity from our accounts seriously distorts our measures of a most profound change in the U.S. economy over the past half-century: the massive movement of women into the labor force, demonstrated graphically in Figure 2.1. Before World War II most women worked in market activities, if at all, until they had children (generally at an early age) and perhaps again after children were grown. Now, most women work for wages and salaries.

The movement of large numbers of women into the labor force has greatly increased market output. But has it increased total output as much? If paid child care is substituted for care by the mother in the home, is that a net increase in child care or output? If restaurant meals are substituted for home cooking, is that an increase in product? If women use part of their market income for commuting expenses, does all of their income properly reflect a net increase in well-being or in output?

WORKING WOMEN AND PRODUCTIVITY

Much has been made of declining rates of growth in productivity per labor-hour of work. Women still find themselves generally in lower-pay and hence, by the usual measure, lower-productivity jobs than men. Therefore, as women move into these lower-pay, lower-productivity jobs, they bring down average productivity. But the fact that women choose to move out of the full-time, nonmarket household into market labor suggests that they view the productivity or return of market labor as higher than that of the nonmarket labor they are fleeing. By moving into market work they are raising

Figure 2.1 *Labor Force Participation Rates, 1948–1992*

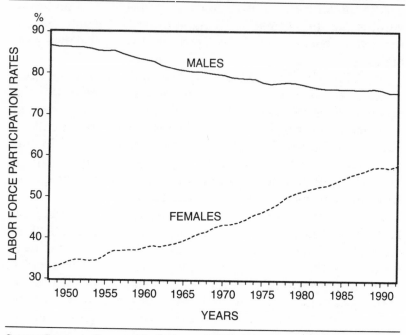

Source: *Economic Report of the President,* 1993, Table B-34, p. 387.

their own productivity. How can this bring down—or even slow the growth of—productivity overall?

To illustrate with numbers, suppose the average wage and productivity per hour in market work is $10 and the wage and productivity of new female entrants to market work is $8 but the (unpaid) value of household work is $5 per hour. Do women entering the labor force really bring down average productivity by adding their $8 jobs to the $10 average? Or do they not raise average productivity of the aggregate of all labor, market and nonmarket combined, by moving from $5 "jobs" in the nonmarket sector to $8 jobs in market activity? The conventional measures, looking only at market labor, declare average worker productivity is declining or growing very slowly. A measure including market and nonmarket labor would put productivity growth in a more positive light.

THE FULL VALUE OF GOVERNMENT OUTPUT

Many may argue that much government output is worthless. They do not wish to credit government bureaucrats with contributing anything to GDP. But they would be reflecting the kind of value judgment that national income counters seek to avoid. It would appear more objective to count the services produced by capital and labor, whether their production is brought on by private market purchases or by the decisions of the people through their government.

We do therefore seek to include a measure of government services in gross domestic product. But since government does not generally sell its services, national accounting practice is to evaluate them on the basis of the cost of their inputs, purchases that are not resold, and hence final product. Since government, however, is not in the business of acquiring capital to earn profit, we do not have profits as a measure of the cost of capital services. With no separate capital accounts for government yet in the BEA NIPAs, we do not include depreciation charges either as a measure of capital services. And with the exclusion of government interest payments from national income we also rule them out as, at least in part, a measure of return to government capital. The only input taken as a measure of government output is labor.

The value of public education services to our children in the official accounts is therefore the salaries and wages paid to school personnel—teachers, administrators, and maintenance workers. If public education were sold in the market by a business, the price would have to reflect the interest or other costs of the financial capital invested, depreciation of school plant and equipment, and, at least for schools for profit, a reasonable net income. The value of education, police, defense, and all other services provided by government includes, however, only their market component, what is paid in wages and salaries to government employees.

When we cut government employment to reduce the deficit, what is a correct measure of the value of the government services we lose? Is it only the wages and salaries of those laid off? Or should it properly include an imputation for the value of capital services of the bases, schools, and equipment that the discharged workers are no longer using?

A FULLER MEASURE OF THE COSTS— AND BENEFITS (?)—OF EDUCATION

In principle, in a free-market economy, the value of output is equal to its cost of production, including an allowance for competitive return on capital or profit. But again relevant are opportunity costs, the values of the opportunities foregone in undertaking any activity. Thus the cost of buying and reading this book is not only the dollars of its purchase price but also the value of the time spent in reading it, or of the alternative use of that time. This book should then be purchased and read only if the value of the return received, in enjoyment and enlightenment, exceeds or is at least equal to the total cost of the book, including not only the purchase price but its full opportunity cost.

Over the years, to illustrate this point, I have asked my students what they take to be the cost of their expensive education at Northwestern University. Is it merely the high tuition? Or does it include what they might have earned in a job during the four years they attend the university? Clearly it is both. Should we not assume that our students know what they are doing and in spending four years in the university have implicitly placed a value on those four years at least equal to these costs? They and their parents must certainly recognize these foregone earnings in balancing costs against the added expected future incomes (and other benefits) associated with a university education. Should not the "output" of the university be valued to reflect them?

In general, our measure of the value of education of those old enough to be in the labor force should include these foregone student earnings. If it did, the economic cost and value of higher education would show up significantly higher than the amounts recorded in the conventional official accounts.

OTHER IMPLICATIONS OF IGNORING NONMARKET OUTPUT

There are other discrepancies between the market value of output and its worth reflecting a correct valuation of all inputs. One relates to volunteer services, in schools, churches, hospitals, and a host of nonprofit enterprises. We attribute no income to volunteers, and since they are costless, the value of their input does not enter into the market price of the output to which they are contributing.

We have an analogous problem with regard to those who are conscripted to service. During the days of the military draft in the United States, should we have counted only the relatively token pay and allowances to draftees as the cost and value of input to military services? Or should we have counted their opportunity cost, the civilian earnings they forfeited when they were forced into military service? Or should we have included the frequently much greater amount, particularly during the unpopular Vietnam War, that the armed forces would have had to pay if they had been forced to hire personnel in a free market, as did defense plants or any other firms? Of much smaller magnitude, but raising the same issue, is the cost of jurors who are forced to serve at a pay that is generally much less than it would take to hire them in a free market.

The failure to take into account nonmarket activity may also lead to exaggerating the losses from cyclical unemployment and the extent that recessions cause a reduction in output. If laid-off workers devote more of their time to repairing the roof, painting the house, and caring for the children, it implies a partial offset to the loss of output occasioned by their absence from the workforce. I would not use this argument to condone policies that bring on or cause increases in unemployment, but our analysis should not ignore this factor.

ACCOUNTING FOR THE ENVIRONMENT

There are other revisions or additions to the conventional accounts that might well be in order. Of particular interest is the handling of the environment. In the conventional accounts, if government undertakes expenditures to combat pollution or protect the environment, they are counted in gross domestic product in accordance with the rule that all government purchases constitute final product. Consumer expenditures for energy made more expensive by environmental protection regulations would increase the nominal or dollar value of personal consumption expenditures and hence of gross domestic product. They would not, however, increase the real value of this final product because only its price, not its quantity, had changed.

Similarly, the increased input to and expense of automobiles necessary to meet more rigorous emission standards may improve the environment. But they will not add to gross domestic output unless they are recognized as an increase in the quantity—or quality—of final product, which in the official accounts in this case is automobiles and not better air; the BEA did not always but does now view emission devices as quality improvement in automobiles. In general, expenditures or output directed at improving the environment will not contribute to real GDP unless they are business physical capital expenditures, are sold to government, or become separately identifiable final product purchased by consumers.

While output directed at protecting or improving the environment is treated quite inconsistently in the conventional accounts, the deterioration or using up of the environment is not counted at all. We might well have a depreciation or "consumption of environment" deduction to match the "consumption of fixed capital" item in our accounts, but we don't.

And we might have an environment investment component of gross private domestic investment. The conventional measure of net private domestic investment presumably tells us how much we are adding to our private stock of capital in the form of houses and business and nonprofit plant and equipment. Net investment in the environment—the difference between expenditures to protect and improve the environment and the current consumption of our environmental resources—would be a measure of whether we are leaving a more or less habitable planet for our children and grandchildren.[8]

A FULLER MEASURE OF SAVING AND INVESTMENT

Of critical importance in formulating and evaluating economic policy must be its effects not merely on current output and welfare but on capital and investment, broadly construed, and hence on the true national saving that will determine our future well-being. This suggests the need for upgrading and extension of the conventional accounts, to sep-

---

[8] A White House release in connection with President Clinton's Earth Day address on April 21, 1993, declared:

> Our economic statistics measure virtually everything except the value of our natural resources and the environmental costs of our actions. President Clinton has directed the Bureau of Economic Analysis to develop "Green GDP" measures to improve existing statistics that ignore the cost of pollution or the value of clean air. These "Green GDP" measures would incorporate changes in the natural environment into the calculations of national income and wealth.
> The existing national income accounting system—used here and in other countries essentially ignores the impact of economic development on the environmental resources that are the foundation of long-term prosperity. The current accounts provide mixed signals: For example, an oil tanker spill can increase GDP if the cost of cleanup is included as income to workers while the pollution costs of fouling the beach go unrecorded.

In response, the BEA has set forth a program to implement the presidential directive and announced: "Within one year the Bureau of Economic Analysis will publish initial estimates of natural resource depletion. After a period of discussion and review, BEA will augment their regular indicator series to include a consistent set of natural resource adjustments."

arate properly all investment from current consumption of goods and services.

In the U.S. government accounts we currently recognize no capital expenditures or investment at all. Most other developed countries do. In accordance with the United Nations System of National Accounts guidelines, which the Bureau of Economic Analysis is committed to follow more closely (if budget cuts do not deprive it of the personnel to undertake the necessary extensions of our existing accounts), the United States will eventually separate government consumption expenditures and investment in structures and equipment.

We classify all household expenditures, except those for new houses, as consumption, although it might be argued that the purchase of durable goods by households is as much an investment in future services as are such purchases by business. After all, does it make sense to count the purchase of a new car by Hertz as investment and the purchase of the same car by an individual as consumption? If that individual were to buy a car from Hertz instead of renting it, the conventional measure of net investment would be reduced by the amount of the sale and the measure of consumption would be correspondingly increased.

And nowhere, in the official conventional accounts of government, business, nonprofit institutions, or households do we count as investment what is perhaps the most important investment of all—the one we make in the intangible capital of education and research that adds to our abilities and stock of knowledge for future production.

Our conventional or "official" national income and product accounts, as they now stand, go a long way toward offering measures of the economy's contribution to well-being, particularly in market activity. Their framework offers a base for evaluation of government policies which is usually ignored at considerable loss.

Yet, to get a fuller picture of where we are headed, it is important to look beyond the official accounts. This is vital in measuring activity not covered in market transactions, largely in households and in government. And it is vital to obtaining a meaningful picture of the totality of saving and investment on which our future depends.

CHAPTER 3

Saving for a Brighter Day

"The public debt on the first day of July last, as appears by the books of the treasury, amounted to $1,740,690,489.49. Probably, should the war continue for another year, that amount may be increased by not far from five hundred millions. Held as it is for the most part, by our own people, it has become a substantial branch of national, though private, property. For obvious reasons, the more nearly this property can be distributed among all the people the better. . . . The great advantage of citizens being creditors as well as debtors, with relation to the public debt, is obvious. Men can readily perceive that they cannot be much oppressed by a debt which they owe to themselves."—Abraham Lincoln, 1864 Annual Message to Congress.[1]

"No State in the world has less need than the United States to make sacrifices for a rapid reduction of the Debt, since in no other State will the Debt so surely and rapidly reduce itself by the growth of the nation."—R. Dudley Baxter, in *National Debts,* 1871, p. 31.[2]

"America has thrown itself a party and billed the tab to the future."[3] We have been on a consumption binge. We have been eating our seed corn. We have been mortgaging

---

[1] From Roy P. Basler, ed., *The Collected Works of Abraham Lincoln* (New Brunswick, N.J.: Rutgers University Press, 1953), vol. 8, pp. 142–143. Quoted in James D. Savage, *Balanced Budgets and American Politics* (Ithaca and London: Cornell University Press, 1988), p. 128.

[2] Quoted in Savage, *Balanced Budgets and American Politics,* pp. 136–137.

[3] Benjamin Friedman, *Day of Reckoning* (New York: Random House, 1988), p. 4.

our future. To widely repeated statements like these, hard-pressed "middle-class" Americans, and certainly the poor, may well retort incredulously, "Who, me?" They feel put-upon or long-suffering and hardly recognize themselves as living high off the hog.

We are not saving enough. That is the charge of the day, or decade, the reason or the excuse for advocating tax cuts and tax increases, capital gains tax relief and investment tax credits, cuts in government expenditures and more government investment, deregulation and industrial policy. To what extent, if at all, is the charge true? And what, if anything, should we do about it?

WHAT WE ARE TALKING ABOUT—INDIVIDUAL SAVING AND NATIONAL SAVING

We should begin by defining what we are talking about. What is saving for the individual? What is saving for the nation?

An individual saves by spending less than his or her income after taxes. That immediately suggests *two* ways of increasing saving: cutting spending *or raising income*.

If income is measured comprehensively, to include everything that contributes to wealth—capital gains as well as wages, salaries, interest, and dividends—saving is the net addition to wealth or net worth. Thus, if we have a yearly income of $50,000, pay taxes of $10,000, and spend $35,000 as a consumer, we have saved $5,000. If we start the year with a wealth or net worth of $100,000, this brings our net worth at the end of the year to $105,000.

What the individual does not spend, but saves, he or she can put under the mattress. It can also be "deposited," in effect lent to a bank, or lent to someone else—to a business by buying its bond or to the government by buying its bond, note, or "bill." The saver can also put money into a pension fund, buy stock in a business, put it into his or her own business, use it to buy a house, contribute to the down payment on a house, or pay off a preexisting debt.

What is common about all of these forms of saving is that the individual acquires a claim to money or an asset that can be used in the future to increase net worth, either by adding to assets or reducing liabilities. The act of saving puts the saver in the position to consume more later. By suffering the pain of cutting current consumption, the saver can realize the gain of consuming more in the future. And indeed if there is a net return to saving, in the form of interest, dividends, profits, or capital gains, cutting current consumption by, say, another $5,000 will permit an increase in future consumption of more than $5,000. There may then be a net gain for the pain of current sacrifice.

But let us suppose that an individual does decide to cut consumption in order to increase saving. Trips to the barbershop or hairdresser go by the board, as does eating out. Relaxation at home may replace going to a golf or tennis resort at vacation time. Our individual's saving goes up, as we have noted. But what happens to the saving of the barber or hairdresser, the restaurant owner and workers, and the golf or tennis pro and other workers in the forsaken resort? Their incomes go down, perhaps by the full amount that an individual increases his saving. If their income goes down by $5,000 and their consumption stays the same, then *their* saving goes down by $5,000. Total saving does not change at all.

Suppose the barber and the others cut their consumption in response to a loss of income. If they cut it dollar for dollar with the loss, their saving does not change. But then still others' incomes go down. And as *they* cut their consumption, new links are added to the income-loss chain.

In fact, our theory and evidence indicate that most people try to maintain some of their consumption as income decreases. At each link in the chain there will be some slippage in saving. In the end, the saving of everybody else may well have declined more than the original increase, so that total saving is decreased![4] Whether or under what conditions this will be so, however, is a key issue I shall be addressing.

---

[4] This phenomenon is known in economics as "the paradox of thrift." Efforts to be thriftier, to save more, cause a reduction in total or aggregate income and hence may even result in less aggregate saving.

If saving consists only of one individual consuming less than income and lending the difference to another who uses it to consume more than income, there is no change in total consumption. If there is also no change in total income, there is no change in total saving, which is simply income minus consumption.

There is likewise no change in total wealth or net worth. The net worth of the first individual has gone up by the amount of her saving and her loan; she now possesses a new asset in the form of the borrower's note or IOU. But if the borrower spends the proceeds of the loan in increased consumption, his saving goes down and his net worth is lowered by the amount of his new IOU. Individual saving can take the form of accumulation of pieces of paper, dollar bills or stocks or bonds. But these paper assets are others' liabilities or are assets acquired at the expense of others. Corresponding to each act of saving, then, is another act of dis-saving. National saving can only occur if the addition to assets of one individual is not the loss of assets or the increase of liabilities of another.

This means that national saving can occur only if we acquire assets that are real domestic assets—new factories, stores, and office buildings, new machinery and equipment, new houses—or new net claims on the rest of the world.

SAVING AND INVESTMENT—YOU CAN'T HAVE ONE WITHOUT THE OTHER

The first set of tangible items constitutes what are called in the national accounts "gross private domestic investment." The second makes up "net foreign investment." The total of the two is gross investment, as may be seen in Table 3.1. Gross saving for the nation is thus equal to gross investment, except for a varying "statistical discrepancy" that comes from our inability to gather all the statistics without errors or omissions.[5]

---

[5]Imagine going to everyone in this country who bought anything and asking them

Table 3.1 *Gross Saving and Investment Account, 1992*
(*billions of dollars*)

Gross Private Domestic Investment	796.5	Private Saving	986.9
Net Foreign Investment	−55.1	Personal Saving	238.7
		Business Saving	748.3
		Undistributed Corporate Profits	110.4
		Business Consumption of Fixed Capital	657.9
		Wage Accruals Less Disbursements	−20.0
		Public Saving	−269.1
		Federal Budget Surplus	−276.3
		State and Local Surpluses	7.2
		Statistical Discrepancy	23.6
Gross Investment	741.4	Gross Saving and Statistical Discrepancy	741.4

Source: Survey of Current Business, August 1993, Table A, p. 55—Summary National Income and Product Accounts, 1992, Account 5—Gross Saving and Investment Account.

The fact that saving and investment are equal in magnitude is fundamental. Not recognizing it can be a source of grave confusion. But recognizing it and misunderstanding its implications can also lead to profound confusion, fatal to efforts to design sound economic policy.

It is investment that provides for the future. On that issue, if investment is correctly and appropriately defined, there can be no difference. And there can be no investment without saving. We cannot increase investment without increasing saving.

On recognizing this, though, many make the fatal slip. They ask for measures to encourage individuals to divert less of their incomes to consumption and more to saving. It seems simple; if there is more saving, there will have to be more investment. If all individuals save more, or even some individuals save more but none saves less, will not total saving go up? It will, but . . .

The big "but" is that if some save more, they may bring down the incomes and saving of others and thus reduce total saving. The necessary equality between saving and investment should remind us that the measures designed to increase saving will not increase aggregate saving—total saving in the economy—unless they increase aggregate investment. The question then becomes, what will these measures do to increase investment? If they do not increase investment, they will not increase saving. If in fact they bring on a decline in investment, then saving must also decline.

---

how much they bought and going to everyone who sold anything and asking them how much they sold. One person's purchase is another person's sale, so the total of purchases and sales in the country, omitting transactions with foreigners, must be equal. It is almost unimaginable, though, that in a survey of 260,000,000 Americans the two totals would in fact prove identical.

Similarly, saving and investment must be equal. The total of saving, however, comes from those who do the saving, those who spend less than their income. The total of investment comes from the data of business and nonprofit institution acquisition of structures and equipment, business additions to inventories, and individuals' acquisition of new houses. Given the enormous problems of collecting accurate information on all this, it would be a miracle if the two totals were precisely equal. Hence the statistical discrepancy.

CUTTING CONSUMPTION MAY NOT RAISE
NATIONAL SAVING

Suppose President Clinton were to launch a major campaign to increase saving. Suppose he were to persuade Americans to cut consumption by $500 billion. One might conclude that, since saving equals income minus consumption, if incomes remain the same, the $500 billion reduction in consumption will mean a $500 billion increase in saving. But remember, there can be no increase in saving without an increase in investment. How will a massive cut in consumption affect investment?

Some of us may cut consumption by not buying new cars. If we do not buy new Chryslers, what will that do to investment by the Chrysler Corporation? If it finds its sales declining, will it build new facilities to expand its plant? Or will it slash plans for such expansion?

My own studies and those of virtually everybody else show that a major factor in business investment, probably the dominant one, is the need to provide facilities to meet the pressure of sales on capacity. A more rapidly increasing demand for product generates more business investment. A mere decline in the rate of increase in demand for product reduces business investment.

Firms do not require as much in the way of new plant and equipment if the physical volume of their sales is growing at 2 percent instead of 4 percent. An actual decline in sales is a disaster for investment. During the Bush administration, as the growth in real consumption ceased and consumption actually declined slightly, gross private domestic investment in constant (1987) dollars fell from (an annual rate of) $803 billion in the first quarter of 1989 to $660 billion by the second quarter of 1991.

If holding back or actually reducing consumption reduces investment, it must reduce saving. How is that possible, since saving equals income minus consumption? The answer should be obvious by now. Consumption goes down but income goes down more. Those people losing jobs and income because investment goods production is down by $135 billion have less income and consume *and save* less. And, as we have seen, as they consume less there is a loss in income by others who were producing the goods and services they are no longer buying.

Investment must equal saving. But it is more informative to say that saving must equal investment. If investment declines by $135 billion, saving must decline by $135 billion. This means that, whatever the decline in consumption, income must decline by $135 billion more than the fall in consumption. Income changes become in effect the instrument and the balancing item to realize the saving-investment equality.

Saving may indeed not come down immediately as we reduce consumption. For example, when people stop buying Chrysler cars, the dealers and then the Chrysler Corporation accumulate unsold automobiles. They have in fact invested, however disagreeably, in additional inventory. That unwanted investment corresponds to increased saving.

But automobile dealers quickly tell the manufacturer that they cannot accept more cars. The manufacturer cuts production and lays off workers. With fewer cars produced, inventories stop piling up and may even decline if output is reduced by more than the decline in sales. The unwanted investment in inventories goes back to zero or becomes negative. And the other side of the lower investment coin is that Chrysler's profits and its workers' incomes are down—or nonexistent—which means that their saving is down. President Clinton's successful appeal to the nation to cut consumption is perverse in its effects. Consumption is down, but so is saving and investment.

Realistically, President Clinton will probably not appeal to the public to lower consumption. Such an appeal would not be likely to be any more effective than a plea for us to follow the example of the 14-year-old boy who voluntarily sent a check for $1,000 to reduce the deficit. Despite all the publicity of that episode, little in the way of such voluntary contributions, or voluntary reductions in consumption, is to be expected.

TAXES AND TAX INCENTIVES FOR SAVING

There are, however, more persuasive means at the disposal of the government. One, offering tax incentives for saving, was actively pursued by Secretary of the Treasury Lloyd Bentsen when he was the powerful chairman of the Senate Finance Committee. It provided tax savings to people who put more money into their pensions or IRAs (individual retirement accounts). The inducement of tax reductions, it was thought, would increase saving. But as we have seen, it could do so only if it cut consumption without cutting income by as much or more. Selling stocks or bonds, rather than reducing consumption, in order to put more money into IRAs or other pension funds clearly will not raise saving.

The government has, however, still more persuasive means at its disposal to induce us to cut consumption. If it raises taxes, we will have less available for spending and we will consume less. This is readily apparent if income taxes are increased. But essentially the same thing occurs if there are increased taxes on our purchases—of energy or alcohol or tobacco. Either we consume less of the things that are taxed or we have less left to spend on other things, or both. Consumption will be down, but in this instance saving will not be up. It is more likely to be down because our real income after taxes, the purchasing power of our income after taking into account the increased taxes to be paid, will be down, and probably down by more than our reduction in consumption.[6]

---

[6]This would be consistent with a central proposition of modern economics: that the "marginal propensity to consume," the fraction of a dollar by which real consumption would change with a one-dollar change in real income, is greater than zero but less than one. Since saving equals income minus consumption, if consumption goes down by less than a dollar when income goes down by a dollar, saving must also decline

Government *dis*-saving—the deficit—is lowered, however, by the amount of the increase in tax receipts. Supporters of higher taxes argue that the reduction of government dis-saving will exceed the reduction in private saving and that total saving therefore will be higher. Whether that will be true is again a question of its effect on investment.

"DON'T RAISE TAXES—CUT SPENDING!"

It is widely argued that while higher taxes may have some of the perverse effects described, deficit reduction by means of cuts in government outlays will increase private investment and national saving. This argument has been repeated so often and has such apparent appeal to self-interest that it is rarely challenged. To Republican and conservative Democratic politicians it has become an article of faith. The Clinton administration's response to the call for greater cuts in spending has been to ask for "specifics" or "details." And where, they ask further, would additional cuts be both feasible and fair to those affected?

Yet the argument that spending cuts would generally be beneficial while tax increases would prove perverse does not readily stand up to scrutiny. Indeed, the difference between cuts in government spending and increases in taxes is in considerable part a matter of semantics, rather than economics, as argument over President Clinton's 1993 economic package should have made clear. The Clinton administration, following the practice of previous administrations, particularly that of Ronald Reagan, chose to classify increased taxes on social security benefits as expenditure cuts, presumably on the ground that they amounted to a reduction in the net outlays for social security. Increases in various user fees for govern-

---

with a decline in income. The corollary to the proposition about the marginal propensity to consume is therefore that the "marginal propensity to save," the fraction of a dollar that real saving would change with a one-dollar change in real income, is also greater than zero but less than one. With a reduction in private real income due to an increase in taxes, private real saving can be expected to decline.

ment services were similarly classified as expenditure cuts, since they reduced the government's net outlays. Critics insisted these should be viewed as increases in taxes or revenues; they were taking more money away from the public.

But imagine two scenarios for a social security recipient. In one, payments are reduced from, say, $10,000 to $9,000. In the other, the government declares that gross payments remain $10,000 but $1,000 is taken out for "taxes." In both cases, net receipts are reduced to $9,000. The only difference is what is written on the stub of the social security check.[7]

Despite all the hullabaloo about reducing "entitlements," rather than increasing taxes, to reduce the deficit, there is no real difference between the two in their effects on purchasing power or the demand for goods. Either will reduce consumption and bring on the chain of events we have described.

However, if increases in taxes entail increases in marginal rates, as they frequently do, we have to consider the argument made by economists who call themselves "supply-siders" and their political allies. They insist that people will be less inclined to supply their labor or capital if the return they can expect from supplying more is reduced, or if the loss suffered from supplying less is reduced. People are thus less inclined to work or to look for profitable investment if net after-tax returns are less. Means-tested entitlements like Medicaid, food stamps, or housing subsidies may also discourage work and the earning of other income.

The supply-side argument that cutting entitlements rather than increasing taxes will make for higher income and

---

[7] I am indebted to Herbert Stein for the following bit of history, which he related in *The Wall Street Journal*, February 24, 1993, p. A14.

In the time of Emperor Vespasian, the government provided urinals in the streets of Rome and charged a fee for their use. The emperor, seeking to reduce his budget deficit, decided to raise the fee. His son, a finicky fellow, asked the emperor whether the additional receipts should be considered a tax increase or a reduction of government expenditures for the provision of the facilities. To this the emperor made his famous reply (in Latin, the only language he spoke): "Non Olet!" The literal translation is, "It doesn't smell." But the meaning is, "It's all money, and it doesn't matter which side of the ledger you put it on."

greater economic well-being may, in principle, have some substance. But while such a choice may increase the size of the economic pie, it may also cause the pie to be carved up in a manner some would consider less equitable.

Lower entitlements would generally injure the poor and those frequently unable to help themselves, as well as the elderly, both middle income and poor. On the other hand, higher taxes, if focused largely on the rich, would not appear to reduce their well-being much. For those who already have everything, having a bit less may not prove very painful.

And further, it is possible to increase taxes and devise entitlements that minimize the disincentives to work and earn income. On the tax side this would mean reducing exemptions, deductions, and credits, thus increasing the amount of income subject to taxation but leaving unchanged or even reducing the marginal rates (the shares taken in taxes from the additional dollars of income earned from more work or more investment). On the entitlement side, it means less in the way of means-tested benefits and more in the way of encouragements to work, such as more generous earned-income tax credits to raise the after-tax income of low-wage workers, turning welfare as far as possible to work-fare, and making quality child care available to working parents. Some of these reforms may appear to add to current budgetary outlays and hence government budget deficits, but they are likely to more than compensate in future revenues both to those directly affected and to the government.

GOVERNMENT SPENDING FOR GOODS AND SERVICES VERSUS SPENDING FOR NOTHING

More significant economically than the difference between spending and taxing are the differences among kinds of spending. On the one hand the government spends for goods and services; it pays the nation's servicemen and servicewomen, and keeps vast numbers of civilians employed, some 18 percent of all full-time equivalent employees. It also spends for the construction and maintenance of roads and buildings and purchases hundreds of billions of dollars worth of military equipment, transportation vehicles, communications equipment, and other capital goods that would be called investment if acquired by private business. In addition, it spends many billions of dollars annually to finance R&D, in government institutes and commercial as well as nonprofit research institutions, including private universities and hospitals.

On the other hand the government makes what economic accountants refer to as "transfer payments." In general these entail payments to people which require no current work in return. The largest of these programs by far is the Old-Age Survivors and Disability Insurance (OASDI) program of social security. Of major significance as well are other government retirement programs for both military and civilian workers, unemployment benefits, and the huge "welfare" system, particularly Aid to Families with Dependent Children (AFDC), food stamps, medicare health benefits for the aged, and medicaid for the poor. The common characteristic of all these payments is that they are given for nothing. They require no current quid pro quo. One only has to exist and fall within such stipulations of the law as age, status of dependency, or unemployment status to receive payments.

A critical point about transfer payments is that they do not directly command the nation's productive resources. A social security recipient may use her social security income to buy a new car, which encourages production and creates income and employment for others. Or she may decide to save it. If she saves by buying a government savings bond, the payment would have come full circle. It will have no impact on the economy unless perhaps her potential heirs decide to spend more in the knowledge that they will be getting a bigger inheritance.

We can expect recipients of transfer payments to spend some, but not all, of their transfer income. Thus an increase in transfer payments will generate both greater private consumption and greater private saving. The increase in private saving is likely initially to be more than outbalanced by the lesser public saving—greater public dis-saving—entailed in the increase in the budget deficit necessary to finance the increase in transfer payments.[8]

If the greater consumption takes resources away from producing investment goods, total saving and investment must be down. If there are sufficient resources idle and available, the consumption sustained by transfer payments or entitlements may eventually generate more investment, and hence more saving.

Government expenditures for goods and services, however, leave nothing to chance. If government spends to hire workers, they must come from the ranks of those not employed or from other jobs. If the government buys goods or nonhuman services, it puts people to work producing these goods and services. Every dollar of government expenditure for goods and services is a direct addition to gross domestic product— unless the labor or services directed to government come from other purchasers. If the other purchasers are those who would buy new business plant and equipment or new houses, increased government purchases of goods and services reduce private investment and hence private saving. The extent to which this will happen or that investment and saving will be increased will depend upon how much there is in the way of free (unemployed) resources.

Cutting both transfer payments and government expenditures for goods and services has the potential of freeing up resources for private investment—the production of additional plant and equipment and residential housing. Cutting transfer payments, though, is a less certain and less potent tool, limited in its effect to the extent recipients alter their consumption spending as a result. Of course, if the cuts in government expenditure include cuts in government invest-

---

[8] Note that this is consistent with propositions of marginal propensities to consume and save greater than zero but less than one and the opposite movements in response to increases in taxes noted above. Transfer payments may be viewed as negative taxes, with the government giving instead of taking.

ment outlays—for roads, bridges, education, or research—
any increased use of resources to produce private capital
goods may be more than balanced by the loss in public investment.

THE INTEREST RATE TO THE RESCUE

We have, however, not yet come to grips with the critical issue, the existence of a mechanism which will ensure that
the reduction in goods and services going to consumption or
to the government will in fact be offset by increases in investment. If such a mechanism exists—and works—saving will
thus be increased. The mechanism to which economists usually look is the rate of interest, operating automatically or
with pushes from the monetary authority.

The idea, put most directly, is that if the government
spends less or taxes more, it will borrow less. The demand for
credit will then be less. If, even without a change in government spending or taxes, people try to save more out of given
incomes, the supply of credit will be greater. In either event
the cost of credit or borrowing will be less; interest rates will
be lower. Lower interest rates mean a lower cost of capital to
business and thus make it more profitable for business to
invest, that is, to acquire new plant and equipment. They also
make it cheaper for people to buy new homes and so foster
investment in housing. The general easing in credit markets
may also make it easier for private borrowers to obtain funds
even aside from any lowering of interest rates.

It is sometimes further argued that the mere anticipation
in financial markets that government borrowing will be less
in the future will generate an anticipation that interest rates
will be lower in the future. That of course means that bond
prices would be higher in the future.[9] This expectation can

---

[9]The rate of interest on a long-term security is essentially the return on a bond
divided by its price, with the maturity or face value having only a lesser relevance.
The return is usually fixed—as $80 per year on an 8-percent, 30-year ($1,000 princi-

lead to an immediate drop in interest rates, as lenders increase the supply of credit in an effort to take advantage of high current interest rates and low bond prices.[10]

President Clinton in the spring of 1993 was therefore claiming that his mere commitment to a $500 billion reduction in budget deficits and hence in borrowing requirements over five years had contributed to a major reduction in interest rates, which was in turn bringing about a revival of new home sales. This reduction was also, he argued, enabling homeowners to refinance mortgages at lower rates and devote the income freed from mortgage payments to consumer purchases that would stimulate the economy, perhaps in turn also generating more private investment.

The critical question is whether the force of lower interest rates in increasing investment in new business plant and equipment will counteract the force reducing investment that stems from the loss in demand for whatever product the new plant and equipment would produce. Will the enticement of lower mortgage rates be sufficient to stimulate more new home buying in the face of higher income taxes? The latter might reduce the income available to service a mortgage as much as or more than those servicing costs are reduced by the lower rates. Will the lower incomes of federal workers and those with reduced entitlements cause a reduction in the demand for consumer goods which is not overcome by lower interest charges on consumer loans? If consumer purchases are down, will manufacturers, despite lower interest costs, find it advisable to invest in new facilities?

---

pal or maturity value) bond, for instance. If market rates of interest go down in the future, investors will rush to buy these 8-percent bonds until the price is above $1,000 and the ratio of the return to the price is less than 8 percent.

[10] If anticipation that government borrowing will drop, a pronouncement by Federal Reserve chairman Alan Greenspan, predictions of a slower economy, or anything else generates the expectation that interest rates will be lower in the future than expected previously, that then is an expectation that bond prices will be higher in the future. Investors rush to buy bonds now before their prices go up so that they can make a profit on the increase in prices. They in fact do bid prices up and interest rates down immediately, even before the budget deficit and government borrowing are actually reduced or the slower economy materializes.

It might be argued that as long as the deficit reduction package is envisaged for the future but not yet implemented, we may have the best of both worlds. Interest rates fall now in anticipation of deficit reduction later. People increase their spending and businesses increase their investment now in response to the lower interest rates without worrying that in the future their incomes will be less because of higher taxes or lesser government spending. All they will note in this regard is that they are currently still receiving the benefits of the large government outlays, with relatively little taken away in taxes.

It is conceivable that this trick would work, but it presumes a certain inconsistency in people's expectations. Investors in financial markets drive down interest rates now in correct anticipation of the lower government borrowing and slower economy that will accompany future reduction in the deficit. Everybody else, however, ignores the prospect that lower future deficits will reduce the demand for goods and services. This could be a consequence of the government reducing its spending for goods and services directly or the lesser private after-tax incomes resulting from reduced government spending or increased taxes.

The fall in interest rates in the first half of 1993 may have come as a result of the mere enunciation of the Clinton deficit-reduction proposals, since investors anticipate not so much a reduction in government borrowing as an overall reduction in borrowing because of a consequent slowdown in the economy. This would imply that lower interest rates would merely partially offset the fiscal drag on the economy and not reverse it. As of July 1993 that seemed to be what was happening. New housing sales, after a spurt in April, plunged in May, despite the lowest mortgage interest rates in 22 years. Unemployment inched back up to 7.0 percent in June. And the administration lowered its forecast of 1993 growth in real GDP from 3.1 percent to 2.5 percent. Unemployment was back down to 6.7 percent in August but payroll employment dropped as well, as manufacturing activity declined for the third month in a row. Construction spending for July was reported down. Interest rates on the "bellwether" 30-year Treasury bond fell below 6 percent for the first time in a generation—and administration economists lowered their 1993 GDP growth forecast to 2.0 percent. Whether efforts to reduce deficits—either by cutting government spending or raising taxes—actually increase national saving remains an empirical question, on which we can get information both by looking at the present and by examining the past several decades of our history. I shall be doing so in Chapter 5.

A BROADER, MORE RELEVANT VIEW OF NATIONAL SAVING

So far we have considered the current, very narrow, official measure of saving, which corresponds to the very narrow official measure of investment. Gross investment in the national accounts, as may be noted in Table 3.1, is the sum of gross private domestic investment—private additions to structures and equipment and new houses[11]—and net foreign investment.

But if saving is thought of in the relevant economic sense of providing for the future and investment as the production of something, tangible or intangible, that can be used in the future, the official conventional measure of saving is so narrow as to be of quite limited relevance and frequently misleading in its implications for national policy decisions.

Suppose you want to make yourself or your children better off in the future. Would it be best to try to maximize current income and minimize consumption, thus achieving the greatest possible rate of saving as currently measured? Or might you be better off going to college instead of working full-time, or borrowing to pay the children's tuition at a good college? Either of these actions would reduce saving as conventionally measured, by reducing current income and/or increasing ex-

---

[11] Plus business additions to inventories.

penditures. But might they not provide more in future income, for yourself or your children, than saving the money and putting it in a money market fund at 3 percent?

If a new car is produced and goes to an automobile dealer who rents it to you, that counts as investment and hence as saving. But, as pointed out in Chapter 2, if you decide it is more economical to buy than enter into a long-term lease, your purchase is counted as consumption and there is no business investment, and thus no saving. It is the same car put to the same use, providing transportation services for a number of years into the future. But in the one instance it is investment and in the other consumption. For many economic purposes, that makes little sense.

Further, if you acquire a new dishwasher, stove, refrigerator, washing machine, or clothes dryer with a new house, that appliance, like the house, is counted as investment. If you buy these "durable goods" separately, they are consumption. In the one case you are said to have saved some of your income and invested it in the appliances that came with the house. In the other, you have gone on that "consumption binge" which keeps down national saving! Yet in both cases the substance of your actions is the same: you are providing for future services.

If United Airlines buys a new plane, that is investment. If Chicago builds a new runway for that plane to land on, that outlay is considered "government expenditure" and is counted, implicitly if not explicitly, as consumption. Similarly, a new truck purchased by business is investment. The highway that is constructed for it to ride on—unless a rare private toll road—is not. If the Internal Revenue Service spends $100,000,000 for new computers to process tax returns, that is not investment. If individual taxpayers buy new computers and software for preparing their returns, that is not investment. If business firms buy new computers, for whatever purpose, that is investment.

The problem here, noted in Chapter 2, is that the conventional U.S. national income and product accounts do not classify government expenditures for durable goods or structures or household expenditures for durable goods as investment. And indeed, the Office of Management and Budget and the Congressional Budget Office do not, except in occasional appendices, separate out capital expenditures. Thus government and household outlays all reduce measured saving, public and private, regardless of what they are for. In Table 3.2, I present separate current and capital government receipts and expenditures accounts. They show that in 1992 $530 billion, or 25 percent of total government expenditures of $2,118 billion, could be deemed capital expenditures. It may also be noted that in a world of trillions, the current account for federal, state, and local governments combined showed a deficit of only $97 billion.

IS IT INVESTMENT IF YOU CAN'T TOUCH IT?—INTANGIBLE INVESTMENT

Even in the business sector, which accounts for the great bulk of gross private domestic investment, important provision for the future is omitted from the totals of investment. In particular, the acquisition of physical R&D facilities or equipment is counted as investment. All the current expenditures for wages, salaries, and other costs of research are merely listed as business expenses. As such they do not even get counted in real gross domestic product. Greater current business outlays for R&D might raise the price of the product and thus increase nominal GDP, but that increase would be counted as "inflation" and not real output.

Research expenditures of nonprofit private universities or institutes, other than those for capital equipment, would in fact be counted, along with other nonprofit institution current outlays, as consumption. The research outlays by public universities or the Office of Naval Research or government agricultural experimental stations or the Department of Energy or the National Institutes of Health are all counted simply as government expenditures for goods and services.

Using up our known reserves of oil and other natural re-

Table 3.2 *Government Receipts and Expenditures Account, 1992 (billions of dollars)*

		Current Account
Credits: Revenues		1,849.4
Charges: Current Expenditures		1,946.1
Goods and Services		601.8
Total	1,131.8	
Minus Cap. Exp.	530.0	
Net Interest, Transfer		986.7
Payments, and Other		
Consumption of Capital		357.6
Surplus or Deficit (−)		− 96.7
		Capital Account
Credits: Consumption of Capital		357.6
Tangible	135.4	
Intangible	222.2	
Charges: Gross Capital Expenditures		530.0
Tangible	196.7	
Intangible	333.3	
Education	261.7	
R&D	71.6	
Net Capital Expenditures		172.4
Surplus or Deficit (−)		− 172.4
		Consolidated Account
Revenues		1,849.4
Expenditures		2,118.5
Total Surplus or Deficit (−)		− 269.1

Sources: National Income and Product Accounts, *Survey of Current Business,* September 1993, Tables 3.2 and 3.3, p. 12, Federal and State and Local Government Receipts and Expenditures, respectively; Tables 3.15, 3.16, and 3.17, pp. 30, 32, 34, "Government Expenditures by Function," "Federal Government Expenditures by Type and Function," and "State and Local Government Expenditures by Type and Function"; Bureau of Economic Analysis, from John Musgrave, "Fixed Government Capital (including residential) historical-cost valuation, gross investment, depreciation and net investment," total; National Science Foundation/SRS, *National Patterns of R&D Resources: 1992,* Tables B-2 and B-3, pp. 47, 48, and data and estimates from Carol Evans of Bureau of Economic Analysis; consumption of intangible capital assumed equal to two-thirds of gross intangible capital expenditures.

sources counts as consumption or as an intermediate product in some other output, but not as disinvestment. The discovery of new reserves is not counted as investment. Using up the environment is not counted as disinvestment or consumption of capital. Expenditures to protect the environment, except to the extent they are expenditures for structures and equipment by business or nonprofit institutions, are not counted as investment.

And perhaps most important of all, the hundreds of billions of dollars—not necessarily enough—spent on education are not counted as investment. Yet what can be more important for future productivity and income than the provision of a well-educated and well-trained labor force? Again, public education outlays fall into that catchall category of government expenditures for goods and services. Outlays by individuals and noncapital outlays of nonprofit institutions are classified as consumption.

It may well be argued that the saving measured in the official conventional accounts (which receives almost all the attention of those expressing concern about low rates of national saving) is but the tip of the iceberg. In Table 3.3, I present an extended gross saving and investment account for 1992 that includes government investment, both tangible and intangible. The addition of $530 billion of "gross public domestic investment" raises the total of gross investment by more than 71 percent. This account still excludes household investment and intangible business investment, however. I have estimated elsewhere that net private domestic investment of the official accounts is no more than 21 percent of appropriately defined, fully comprehensive net capital accumulation in the U.S. economy.[12]

---

[12]See my *The Total Incomes System of Accounts* (Chicago: University of Chicago Press, 1989), "Extended Accounts for National Income and Product," *Journal of Economic Literature*, December 1988, pp. 1–78, and "The Real Rate of U.S. National Saving," *The Review of Income and Wealth*, series 37, no. 1, March 1991, pp. 1–18.

Table 3.3   *Extended Gross Saving and Investment Account, 1992*
(*billions of dollars*)

Gross Private Domestic Investment	796.5	Net Private Saving	329.0
		Personal Saving	238.7
Gross Public Domestic Investment	530.0	Business Saving	90.3
Net Foreign Investment	−55.1	Net Public Saving	−96.7
		Consumption of Capital	1,015.5
		Private (Fixed)	657.9
		Public	357.6
		Statistical Discrepancy	23.6
Gross Investment	1,271.4	Gross Saving and Statistical Discrepancy	1,271.4

Sources: Table 3.2, above, and *Survey of Current Business,* August 1993, Table A, p. 55—Summary National Income and Product Accounts, 1992, Account 5—Gross Saving and Investment Account.

WHAT DIFFERENCE DOES IT MAKE?

Focus on a full measure of saving and investment drastically alters the basis for public policy debate. As I have suggested, it can be argued that raising taxes may bring an increase in the narrow measure of saving if the consequently lower consumption is channeled, via lower interest rates, into more investment. I have maintained that this is questionable, because lower sales by business, as a consequence of reduced consumption, are likely to depress business investment more than the lower interest rates may increase it.

With a comprehensive view of saving and investment, we have to ask whether increased taxes may not also depress individual or household investment in durable goods. Fewer automobiles owned by individuals mean as much in the way of reduced transportation services in the future as fewer automobiles owned by Hertz. And if higher taxes (or higher tuition and fees in public universities) make it impossible to go to college or send our children there, the deck would seem all the more stacked against raising taxes to increase provision for the future.

What about cutting government expenditures to free resources directly, or reducing the deficit and lowering interest rates to bring about an increase in private investment? However this might work with regard to the narrow measure of investment, suppose the cuts in government expenditures are cuts in public investment for roads, bridges, airports, and infrastructure in general? What if the cuts are in research expenditures, which constitute reductions in investment under our comprehensive measure and which also may be critical to private investment in new technology? What if the cuts are in support for Head Start programs for small children, apprenticeships for those in secondary schools, or the financing of higher education?

The comprehensive measures of saving and investment suggest that many of the recommendations inspired by the conventional wisdom of those who would increase saving are very wide of the mark. What really counts is not the size of the deficit or the amount of private saving as currently measured. What is critical is what households and business and government are spending for. It makes a big difference if individuals turn out to be big borrowers and spenders to gamble in Las Vegas or to buy durable goods or new houses or finance their children's education. It makes a big difference if business spends on competitive advertising and plotting new leveraged buyouts or on research to develop better products and better processes of production. And it makes a big difference if government spends on stationing troops in Europe or supporting investment in people and new technology at home.

TODAY VERSUS TOMORROW—MUST WE ALWAYS CHOOSE?

No free lunch! That is almost a watchword of our dismal science. With regard to saving and investing for the future, that translates into a warning that we have to sacrifice current joys and hold back the resources that are contributing to them if we wish to apply more resources to producing the capital that will make us better off in the future. This applies, it will be noted, to all kinds of investment—in business plant and equipment, public education, and research in high-powered government or private institutes. For economists it is elementary that resources are limited, and a large part of our discipline is devoted to learning and advising how best to make use of the limited resources we have. More for one thing presumably means less for another.

It is this concept, of course, that is lurking behind much of the discussion in the pages above. To provide more for the future, many argue, we must limit what we take in the present. Government itself must take less, by commanding fewer goods and services. And government must discourage the private sector from taking too much by reducing entitlements and by raising taxes.

For those who see our economy as generally or "in the long

run" operating at the limits of its capacity, the law of scarcity dominates. It may well be conceded that periods can arise when the amount of free resources is clearly less than the requirements for some recommended new initiative. This has seemed to occur when the new initiative involved major military action, such as World War II and probably Vietnam, but not Grenada, Panama, or the brief Persian Gulf War.

The last, largely financed by U.S. allies, points up the fact that even if resources are scarce, a significant amount of domestic investment can be—and has been for most nations, including our own—financed by foreign investment. But in general, it seems hard to dispute the fact that for most of the past century the U.S. economy has been marked by an abundance of resources, human and physical, that were not in full use. Increases in consumption were usually not at the expense of investment but accompanied by more investment.

Building more roads (investment) led to more driving (consumption). Private investment booms have fueled, not discouraged, consumption "binges." Social security benefits certainly have fostered consumption among the elderly, but they have also brought huge investments in retirement communities across the nation. Medicare, whatever the excesses, inefficiencies, or lacks in our national health program, has certainly contributed not only to current health care but also to investment in the most advanced technology in the world. And as we shall see, public spending and deficits, contrary to popular notions, may generally have contributed to more—if still insufficiently—not less investment in tomorrow.

The choice may not always be so stark. We may be able to have a bigger lunch today *and* tomorrow too. If we pose the choice wrongly, we may suffer pain today for no gain, or even loss tomorrow.

CHAPTER 4

Poor-Mouthing the United States—The United States in the World

". . . [H]ad the Republican principles of balancing the budget been accepted in 1931 and 1932, the final stone in the foundation of permanent recovery would have been laid three years ago instead of deferred for years hence."— Herbert Hoover, after the 29 percent drop in real GNP and increase in unemployment from 3.2 percent to 23.6 percent from 1929 to 1932.[1]

"I have said fifty times that the budget will be balanced for the fiscal year 1938. If you want me to say it again, I will say it either once or fifty times more. That is my intention."—Franklin D. Roosevelt, just before the 5 percent decline in real GNP and increase in unemployment from 14.3 percent to 19.0 percent from 1937 to 1938.[2]

In the 1988 electoral campaign, it rose to a crescendo. The United States had become "The World's Greatest Debtor Nation." We heard it over and over, particularly from Demo-

---

[1] From "Hoover Attacks the Deficits," *The New York Times,* April 10, 1933. Quoted in James D. Savage, *Balanced Budgets and American Politics* (Ithaca and London: Cornell University Press, 1988), p. 168.

[2] From William E. Leuchtenburg, *Franklin Delano Roosevelt and The New Deal, 1932–1940* (New York: Harper & Row, 1963), pp. 37, 45, 48, 91. Quoted by Savage, *Balanced Budgets and American Politics,* p. 170. Savage explains, "Roosevelt was under great pressure from members of the Democratic party, including party leaders Robert Wagner and Bernard Baruch, to balance the budget. 'With the monotony and persistence of old Cato,' declared Baruch, 'we should make one single and invariable dictum the theme of every discourse: Balance budgets. . . . Cut governmental spending—cut it as rations are cut in a siege. Tax—tax everybody for everything.'"

cratic politicians anxious to tie the blame to Reaganomics and the large budget deficit of the Reagan era. Editorialists and economists who should have known better all trumpeted the alarm.[3]

There were many things wrong with the charge, but one stands out: it simply was not true. And after five years of even larger budget deficits and trade deficits, the charge, not heard as often, is still not true in any literal or relevant sense.

In the 1992 campaign we frequently heard Governor Clinton say that the United States had fallen to thirteenth place in the world of real wages. That assertion was based upon a misguided translation to dollars at official or market exchange rates of foreign wages paid in foreign currencies. It too was not true in any relevant economic sense.

Today we are frightened repeatedly by those who warn that for one reason or another we cannot compete with the Japanese, the Koreans, the Chinese, or the Mexicans. We are alternately told that we are losing jobs and the wealth of our nation to the Japanese because they are not permitting free trade, and that we will lose jobs and our prosperity to the Mexicans if we do permit free trade.

A FEW FUNDAMENTALS

In the immortal words of a former president,[4] let me first make one thing "perfectly clear." The United States is by far the greatest economic power on earth. Even at those

---

[3] Witness one of many possible examples, Benjamin Friedman:

> Today, after a half-dozen years in which our government has borrowed record sums on our behalf, we owe foreigners far more than they owe us. The balance against us, already amounting to more than $7,000 per family, now makes the United States the world's largest debtor. Foreigners have already begun to settle these debts by taking possession of office buildings in American cities, houses in American suburbs, farm land in the heartland, and even whole companies. We are selling off America, and living on the proceeds.—*Day of Reckoning* (New York: Random House, 1988), p. 6.

[4] Richard Nixon, of course.

misleading market exchange rates, the total U.S. GDP in
1992 according to OECD (Organization for Economic Cooperation and Development) statistics was 58 percent more than
that of its nearest rival, Japan. In terms of the quantity and
quality of goods and services enjoyed by the people of the two
nations, the gap is much larger. U.S. GDP *per capita* was put
at $22,700 in 1992. That of Japan was estimated at $19,400
and of Germany at $19,900.[5] The OECD put the real per cap-
ita GDP of both Japan and Germany at 87 percent of that of
the United States.

Should we worry about the difficulties of competing with
the rest of the world? The rest of the world has more to worry
about in competing with us. The United States is the world's
greatest exporter, its $636.6 billion in 1992 considerably ex-
ceeding the exports of its closest rival, the new, united
Germany.

As to being thirteenth, or whatever, in real wages, one
would have to look long and hard to find a country where the
average worker finds the *purchasing power* of his or her wages
equal to that of the average worker in the United States. The
craze for shopping sprees by Japanese and Western European
visitors in the United States offers some suggestion as to the
real state of comparative prices. There have been careful studies in recent years comparing wages and national incomes on
a purchasing power basis.[6] The United States, one can be
assured, remains number one among major powers, with Swe-
den and Switzerland probably coming closest, except for a
few oil-rich kingdoms like Kuwait, at least before its recent
occupation by Iraq and subsequent "liberation."

Ross Perot, 1992 independent presidential candidate, warns
of the "sucking sound" of a million U.S. jobs going to Mexico
if the North American Free Trade Agreement (NAFTA) is
ratified. Aside from being a poor prediction with no basis in

---

[5] *New York Times,* July 4, 1993, p. 6.
[6] Most important, by the late Irving Kravis, in association with Robert Summers,
Alan Heston, and Robert Lipsey. These studies compare what the currencies and
incomes of residents of various countries can actually buy.

historical fact, his remarks and others like them betray a fundamental misunderstanding of international economic relations and of the nature of foreign trade. As a matter of fact, Mexican easing of trade barriers over the past several years has contributed to a tremendous export boom for the United States in Mexico, such that we now have a large export surplus with Mexico, the third largest in our bilateral accounts.[7] Those exports may in part entail capital goods that can be used in putting Mexicans to work producing some things currently produced in the United States. But the production of all those goods we export puts hundreds of thousands of Americans to work.

ON LAWYERS, SECRETARIES, AND CANDLE MAKERS—THE LAW OF COMPARATIVE ADVANTAGE

There is a fundamental analytical concept that Ross Perot, some concerned trade unionists, and others ignore at their peril. That is, despite a variety of sophisticated revisions which knowledgeable economists agree does not alter its fundamental conclusions, the "law of comparative advantage," enunciated by the classical English economist, David Ricardo.[8] Economics instructors are fond of setting the stage for teaching this law by exposing students to the satirical "Petition of the Candle Makers,"[9] which beseeched the French Chamber of Deputies for protection from "the intolerable competition of a foreign rival"—the sun!

The law of comparative advantage rigorously demonstrates that trade is a two-way street, the gains from which are in

---

[7] Exceeded in 1992 only by our surpluses with the Netherlands and Belgium-Luxembourg.

[8] In *The Principles of Political Economy and Taxation*, 1817, Chapter VII on foreign trade.

[9] Written in 1845 by the French popularizer of classical economic thought, Frederick Bastiat, published in his *Economic Sophisms* and reprinted in Paul A. Samuelson, Robert L. Bishop, and John R. Coleman, eds., *Readings in Economics* (New York: McGraw-Hill, 1952), pp. 345–347, and in many subsequent editions of the *Readings*.

no way impeded by differences in wages or productivity. It makes clear that a nation with an absolute advantage in the production of all goods should not produce all goods. It should rather specialize in those goods in which it has the greatest absolute advantage, the comparative advantage. It should export these goods in return for imports of goods in which it also has an absolute advantage, but a lesser one. Similarly, the poorer nation will find it advantageous to specialize in the goods in which it has the least disadvantage. It can export those in turn for imports of the goods in which it would have the most disadvantage in domestic production.

The analogy is frequently made to the attorney who is an excellent typist, faster and more accurate than her secretary. It pays the attorney, nevertheless, to leave the typing to her secretary and to concentrate on her legal practice, in which she has a still greater advantage over her secretary than she has in typing. In international trade, the point is that capitalizing on the law of comparative advantage permits greater world output and creates terms of trade where all nations can have more of all goods, those in which they specialize and export and those which they import in return.[10]

---

[10] A contrived but perhaps not wholly inaccurate example may make the principle clear. Assume that the United States has a large advantage over Japan in the production of passenger aircraft, such that 100,000 U.S. workers could produce 100 planes a year in Seattle or elsewhere, while the Japanese would struggle with 100,000 workers to produce 50 comparable planes in a year. Assume (perhaps with less realism) that U.S. auto production is such that 100,000 workers in the U.S. automobile industry can now produce in Michigan (or Kentucky, where Toyota has a plant) 200,000 autos, as against Japanese production of 160,000 similar cars with 100,000 workers. The United States thus has an absolute advantage in the production of both planes and autos, but a greater absolute advantage, two to one versus five to four, that is, a comparative advantage, in planes. Let us compare the production and consumption possibilities first if both nations split 100,000 workers equally between plane and car production.

	U.S.	Japan	Total
Planes	50	25	75
Autos (thousands)	100	80	180

Now suppose that, to the extent tastes permit, free trade induces the United States to shift two-fifths of its workers (and corresponding nonlabor resources) in automobile

MAXIMIZING THE GAINS AND MINIMIZING THE LOSSES

There are some difficulties, as pointed out at the end of note 10. As comparative advantage shifts, obeying its law maximizes production, but that may come at the expense of some workers who lose jobs. It may be at the expense of certain kinds of workers—blue-collar for example, even as engineers and computer specialists may gain. It may be at the expense of industrial workers in general and to the benefit, say, of farmers or operators of financial services.

In a world of free movement of people across international boundaries, newly surplus workers in one industry in one country could in principle move to another country where their industry had moved into comparative advantage and jobs were available. But international migration of labor is frequently barred or severely limited by immigration laws. And for most Americans, certainly, pulling up roots and moving to a country like Japan is hardly a reasonable option.

Further, U.S. auto workers may not be able to preserve their high wages by moving to Japan. Recall that the Japanese may have a *comparative* advantage in automobile pro-

---

production to planes while the Japanese shift three-fifths of their labor and other resources in planes to autos. Output after this specialization will appear as follows.

	U.S.	Japan	Total
Planes	70	10	80
Autos (thousands)	60	128	188

It is quite clear that there are various possible terms of trade—for example, 18 planes for 45,000 cars—that allow the United States and Japan to enjoy both more autos and more planes. For these particular terms, the final picture would be:

	U.S.	Japan	Total
Planes	52	28	80
Autos (thousands)	105	83	188

Consumers in both countries are better off in both products.

There is a little problem, though. Some U.S. automobile workers have lost their auto jobs and some Japanese plane workers have lost their plane jobs. If U.S. auto workers move from Michigan (or Kentucky) to Seattle and take jobs with Boeing and if Japanese workers move from plane production to auto production in Japan, all will be well. The problem, not really so little, is treated in the text below.

duction even with lower absolute productivity and, presumably, lower real wages.

Strong trade unions may be able to keep wages in some industries higher than those in others. And whatever contributes to domestic labor scarcity in an industry may keep its wages high. Without free movement of labor, workers who find themselves in high-wage, scarce-labor positions will face the competition of *products* of labor in less scarce supply and hence receiving lower relative pay. These would come into the market that kept the labor itself out and hence exert downward pressure on wages.[11] If the competition is from the products of foreign labor, the high-wage workers may be able to maintain at least some of their relatively superior position with the imposition of quotas, tariffs, or other protectionist devices, but these will be at the expense of others in the population, including, very likely, other workers.[12]

Major problems with free trade stem from the difficulties of adaptation to change. Free trade adds to the vicissitudes of domestic change and competition the pressures emanating from change in the rest of the world. Automobile and steel workers in Michigan and Ohio who once enjoyed high employment at relatively high wages—high relative to those of other industries *in the United States*—are understandably upset at changes in their fortunes. It is small comfort to them to be told of experienced workers who are doing very well in aircraft in Seattle or in electronics in Silicon Valley. They are likely to offer what political opposition they can to the free competition, international and intranational, that may promote progress at their expense. As they lose their jobs, they

---

[11] The famous Stolper–Samuelson factor-equalization theorem, first enunciated by Wolfgang Stolper and Nobel-laureate (to be) Paul A. Samuelson in their "Protection and Real Wages," *Review of Economic Studies,* 1941, *9,* pp. 58–73.

[12] These costs extend well beyond the usual measures of increased prices paid by consumers. What is not usually recognized is that anything, including protection, which reduces our imports, reduces the supply of dollars on foreign exchange markets, and thus raises the price of the dollar. A higher price of the dollar, though, makes it more difficult for foreigners to buy our goods. We may then find that Japan buys Airbuses in Europe instead of Boeings in Seattle. The workers in General Motors may save their high-wage jobs at the expense of the jobs at the Boeing plants.

also constitute a major waste of resources which the free market often does not readily eliminate. To limit this waste, as well as reduce political opposition to change, it is vital that public policy include measures to move and retrain workers who are victims of change, whether of domestic origin or from abroad.

Free trade need not, as some charge, leave the United States a low-productivity service economy. Services are indeed an increasing part of the U.S. economy and most economies in the world. And services are being provided with greater efficiency; productivity gains in services—including retail and wholesale trade, as well as transportation, financial, electronics, and communications services—may well be our greatest. But as I shall indicate throughout this book, our largest gains in productivity seem likely to come from investment in human capital, in education and training, and in research. Free trade does not mean leaving our population ill-equipped for competition in those industries and activities on the leading edge of modern technology. If we do so, we will still find it advantageous and profitable to trade. But we will then find our comparative advantage in industries where we are less productive, not more productive than the rest of the world. They will be industries in which we are not as much less productive as in the more advanced industries, in which we are further behind. It would be that failure to invest in ourselves, and not free trade, that would threaten us eventually with second-class economic status in the world.

"THE WORLD'S GREATEST DEBTOR NATION"

This charge, still affecting economic policy, merits some consideration as an illustration of lack of knowledge of what counts or how to count it.

First, few seem to recognize the pervasiveness of debt. At the end of 1992, total credit market debt owed by domestic nonfinancial sectors in the United States came to $11.8 trillion, roughly twice the total gross domestic product. Of that debt, little more than one-quarter, or $3.1 trillion, was U.S. government debt. A much larger portion, $8.7 trillion, was private debt. Total liabilities of financial as well as nonfinancial borrowers—including, for example, deposits at financial institutions, which are liabilities of these institutions to their depositors—came to no less than $30.3 trillion. Before we gasp with horror at this "debt," we might pause to note that the totals identified as assets were still greater: $38.3 trillion.[13]

There is nothing necessarily bad about debt. People borrow to buy houses, banks "borrow" our deposits to re-lend them, businesses borrow to invest in new plant and equipment, and governments borrow. And of course, for every borrower there must be a lender. If debt is considered negative by the borrower, it should be viewed as positive by the lender.

If there were no borrowing or lending involving foreigners, the total of borrowing and lending would obviously have to be the same. *Net debt* would be zero. As we shall see in subsequent chapters, this has profound implications, largely misunderstood, for the federal debt about which we hear so much. It means that the great bulk of the $3.1 trillion net debt of the federal government represents net assets of state and local governments and, primarily, of the households, nonprofit institutions, banks, and businesses that constitute the private sector of the economy.

That oft-repeated "World's Greatest Debtor Nation" charge, however, related not to domestic debt but to the debt of Americans to foreigners—or what is designated in official jargon "the rest of the world." And it related in only small part to debt of the *U.S. government* abroad; about $500 billion, an eighth of the total gross federal debt, or 16 percent of the net federal debt held by the public,[14] is held by foreigners. That,

---

[13] Sources for all these numbers: *Federal Reserve Bulletin,* May 1993, "Summary of Credit Market Debt Outstanding and Summary of Financial Assets and Liabilities," Tables 1.59 and 1.60, pp. A42–A43.

[14] The total gross federal debt, approaching $4.4 trillion at the end of the 1993 fiscal

by the way, amounts to less than 2 percent of total U.S. liabilities.

In fact, the so-called debtor status of the United States refers not to "debt" but rather to investments of all kinds. It is the difference, as the U.S Bureau of Economic Analysis measures it, between the value of investments by foreign residents, businesses, and governments in the United States and the value of foreign investments held by the residents, businesses, and government of the United States. Many of these investments are in debt securities, but a substantial amount are in stocks (equity) and in direct investment, whereby companies of one country own all or parts of companies in another.

How does one country undertake net investment in another? Contrary to popular belief, however widely that may be articulated in financial circles that should know better, it is not a matter of "hot money" moving from nation to nation. If a reader decides to buy stock on the Tokyo exchange, she causes no net investment by the United States in Japan. True, she has invested in Japan. But the dollars she has given to get yen with which to acquire Japanese stock—behind-the-scenes transactions about which her broker does not tell her (and may not even know much)—are investments in the United States by the Japanese who acquires the dollars. The United States then invests in Japan while Japan invests in the United States; the two transactions from the standpoint of "debtor" status or net investment are a wash.

---

year, excludes federal securities held by the various government trust funds and some government agencies. What I refer to as the net federal debt, otherwise known as the gross federal debt held by the public, excludes these securities held within the government itself. It is approaching $3.3 trillion at the end of the 1993 fiscal year. It may be noted that this "net" figure still includes some $300 billion of Treasury securities held by the Federal Reserve banks. These are included in the debt "held by the public" because the Federal Reserve banks are technically public corporations, owned by the banks or other depository institutions that are "members" of the Federal Reserve system. The economically most relevant figure of federal interest-bearing debt held by the public would exclude these Federal Reserve bank holdings, so that we would arrive at a figure of just about $3.0 trillion at the end of the 1993 fiscal year.

NET FOREIGN INVESTMENT AND
THE CURRENT ACCOUNT

One country invests in another by selling to it more than it buys. When the Japanese sell us a Sony TV set and we pay, as we usually do, in dollars, the Japanese acquire dollar balances in American banks. In acquiring these dollars they have invested in the United States, initially lending their money to the U.S. banks in which they keep their accounts. Thereafter, they may use the dollars to buy stock or bonds in U.S. companies, to buy U.S. hotels or motels, second homes in Hawaii, Rockefeller Center in New York, or U.S. Treasury securities. But that is a matter of how they arrange their portfolio, the ultimate form of their investments. The Japanese invested in the United States the moment they sold us that Sony.

A country with an excess of imports (purchases) may pay for this excess in its own currency, as is usually the case for the United States. Foreigners, as they are paid, are then investing in the paying country or in the country of whatever currency the paying country is using. If Americans were by chance to use yen—unlikely since they do not hold very many yen—to buy a new car made in Japan, this would constitute disinvestment by the United States in Japan, which is the algebraic equivalent of investment by Japan in the United States.

Net investment, the acquisition of more claims—stocks, bonds, currency, direct investment, whatever—of one country in another must have its counterpart in net exports of something else. Foreigners give us financial claims in return for other things, predominantly goods and services, which we give (sell) them. Net foreign investment is the acquisition by a nation of claims or investments in the rest of the world in excess of the claims foreigners are acquiring on it. One might think that this must be equal to the net exports (exports minus imports) of goods and services that would generate such claims. Close, but not exactly right. Net foreign investment

Table 4.1 *Net Foreign Investment, 1992**

	Billions of Dollars
Receipts from the Rest of the World	769.7
Exports	640.5
Merchandise	448.7
Services	191.7
Receipts of Factor Income	129.2
Payments to the Rest of the World	769.7
Imports	670.1
Merchandise	544.5
Services	125.6
Payments of Factor Incomes	121.9
Transfer payments to foreigners (net)	32.7
From persons (net)	10.4
From government (net)	16.3
From business	6.0
Net Foreign Investment	−55.1

*Adapted from *Survey of Current Business,* September 1993, Table 4.1, p. 14.

equals the net surplus on "current account" (adjusted for certain discrepancies between our balance of payment accounts and the national income and product accounts maintained by the Bureau of Economic Analysis). Exports and imports, of merchandise and services, are major items in the receipts from and payments to the rest of the world, as shown in Table 4.1.

But the complete determinants of net foreign investment are the receipt of funds from exports and factor income (including mainly investment income from the foreign use of our capital) minus the funds used up in imports, in the payment of factor incomes (including the payment of dividends and interest to foreigners for the use of their capital), and in transfer payments. These last would include gifts by Italian-Americans to their relatives in Palermo and social security payments by the federal government to elderly Polish-

Americans who found retirement to be more pleasant or more economical in Warsaw. And the services include transportation and tourist services, as well as services to our troops stationed overseas.

Each year that a nation has positive net foreign investment—a positive current account balance—it is building up the claims of its residents on foreigners more than foreigners are building up their claims on it. In the nineteenth century much of Europe had an export surplus with the United States; its accompanying net foreign investment financed much of the building of the American railroads and the development of our frontier. This put the United States into a net "debtor" status. Foreign claims (investments) in the United States were greater than U.S. claims on foreigners. With World War I, that situation changed abruptly as the warring nations of Europe ran great import surpluses to get the materials for the war, liquidating their U.S. investments to pay for it. That process went much further with World War II, out of which the United States emerged as clearly the world's greatest *creditor* nation.

THE PRESUMED U.S. SHIFT TO "DEBTOR" STATUS IN THE 1980s

In the 1980s the situation changed abruptly. The real, trade-weighted value of the dollar rose some 56 percent from 1980 to 1985. That is to say, compared to what they could buy at home with a U.S. dollar, Americans by 1985 could buy 56 percent more in foreign goods. No wonder that, further fueled by continuing recovery from the deep recession of 1982–1983, large U.S. import surpluses resulted; all manner of imports, very noticeably including Japanese cars and electronics, began to flood American markets.

U.S. net foreign investment figures turned sharply negative, running minus more than $100 billion for each of a number of years, as foreigners acquired dollars in payment for their large net exports to us. The positive net international investment position of the United States, accumulated from years of prior positive net foreign investment, seemed to disappear quickly, as may be noted in Figure 4.1. By 1988 that position—not, it should be noted, the debt position but rather the position in investments of all kinds—had turned, by BEA report, to several hundred billion dollars negative. If the two series were correctly and consistently calculated, repeated large negative net foreign investment would indeed drive our international investment position (or balance) more and more into the red.

Hence the charge that we had irresponsibly let ourselves become the world's largest debtor nation. Our profligacy, by putting us in debt to the rest of the world, would somehow put us, the world's number-one superpower, at the mercy of such countries as Japan, Germany, and England. And it would, if the deficits on current account and negative net foreign investment were allowed to continue, add more and more to the "debt" that future generations would have to service and repay.

Many attributed these current account deficits directly to our federal budget deficits, which were mistakenly understood to entail increasing direct sale of the federal debt to foreigners. Blame for our presumed debtor status is laid on those beyond our shores, and on those at home who do not stand up to the greedy foreigners. The Japanese are accused of keeping our products out and using devious means to undercut us in our own markets. They accumulate U.S. dollars by selling to us. Then, instead of using the dollars to buy our goods and services they use them to acquire our wealth.

To recover from the disaster we were offered remedies: raise taxes, cut spending, sacrifice. Eliminating the budget deficit would eliminate our trade deficit. If a budget surplus brought on a trade surplus, we could begin to reduce both our monstrous domestic debt and our even more monstrous "debt" to foreigners. Getting tough with foreigners and protecting our own markets would further stem the hemorrhage of dollars to the rest of the world.

Figure 4.1 *Net Foreign Investment and International Investment Position of the United States, 1982–1992*

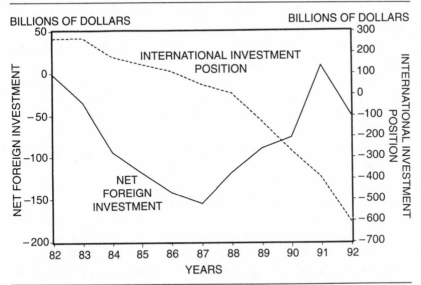

Source: *Economic Report of the President*, 1993, Table B-18, p. 368; *Survey of Current Business*, June 1993, Table 4.1, p. 11; and Russell B. Scholl, Jeffrey H. Lowe, and Sylvia E. Bargas, "The International Investment Position of the United States in 1992," *Survey of Current Business*, June 1993, Table 3, p. 47.

WHAT IS THAT "DEBT"?

In the days when it seemed easier to make the case that budget deficits were benign, it was frequently explained that the resulting government debt consisted of securities held within the nation. The debt was "owed to ourselves." If the government was a debtor, we were all creditors.

If we had no debt to foreigners, then the *net* debt of the United States, as noted above, would always be zero. For every debtor there had to be a creditor. For every dollar of someone's liabilities there was a dollar of someone's financial assets. Consequently, it should have been clear that the more the federal government was a debtor the more the rest of us—state and local governments, businesses, and house-holds—had to be creditors. If owing is bad, is not owing good? For the federal government to reduce its debt is to re-duce the net creditor position of the rest of us. Unless some-thing else compensates, it is to reduce our net worth, our wealth, our accumulated savings.

It is strange that in a society that repudiates totalitarian doctrine, that believes government exists to serve the people and not people to serve the government, so many advocate reducing the government debt at the expense of the people it is to serve. To make the point all the sharper, imagine that the federal government ran budget surpluses so long that it not only had used our taxes to buy back or "pay off" the government debt, but also began using those excess taxes to buy private debt—corporate bonds, home mortgages, and the like. Instead of the government owing us we would owe the government. Instead of the government paying us interest we would pay interest to the government. Would we be better off?

This line of argument, I am frequently told, is irrelevant today, because we owe so much to foreigners. That charge too, as far as it applies to federal government debt, is simply not true. The proportion of the federal debt held by foreigners is small, and is actually smaller than it was a dozen years ago. At the end of the 1992 fiscal year the portion of the total gross public debt that was held by foreigners was 12.3 percent. As a ratio of the smaller gross debt held by the public, the figure was 16.3 percent. The corresponding figures for 1980 were actually a bit more: 13.8 percent and 16.8 percent. The great bulk of the federal debt was then—before the deficits of the 1980s—and is still internally held.

Another point that is widely misunderstood or unrecog-nized is that this debt, relatively small as it is, is all owed in our own currency, U.S. dollars. We pay interest and principal in U.S. dollars. And our Treasury and Federal Reserve can always create all the dollars we need. One may object that such money creation or the monetization of the interest-bearing debt may have undesirable consequences, particularly greater inflationary pressure. But it may also have the desirable effect of stimulating the U.S. economy if that is in order. In any event, the fact that U.S. debt held by foreigners is virtually all denominated in U.S. dollars rules out the possibility of involuntary default on U.S. government obligations.

We are not in the position of many third world or other debtor nations that sadly had obligations in foreign currencies, frequently the U.S. dollar. The only way they could service their debt was to obtain foreign currencies. This could be done by further borrowing, by selling off their assets, or by selling to foreigners more than they bought from them. The last method, usually recommended by the International Monetary Fund and the World Bank, could be painful and damaging. It entailed sacrificing current living standards, foregoing the foreign capital imports needed to invest in their future, or both.

The "world's greatest debtor nation" gave the American public visions of the United States going bankrupt. Since the debt was essentially in our currency, however, this made no sense. We could always "print" our own money to pay it off or, in more sophisticated fashion, have the Federal Reserve create the money.

But nobody stopped to look into the fact, as I have explained above, that the presumed basis for the appellation, "debtor nation," did not relate directly to debt. Actually, it was technically the difference between the measured value of claims by Americans to assets in the rest of the world, and claims by the rest of the world to assets in the United States. These assets included everything: oil wells, motels, factories, stocks, bonds, and bank deposits. Only a portion could be classified as "debt" and, as we have pointed out, virtually all of that portion is denominated in U.S. dollars.

ANOTHER BAD MEASURE

Few looked further into the accuracy and validity of the measure of net claims or "net international investment position" of the United States. In fact, the measure was distorted and invalid, chiefly because important types of investment—most notably, direct investment—were valued (as accountants frequently value things) at original cost. But what is the value of your house, if you bought it 20 or 30 years ago? Is it the value you paid for it—or something else? The current market value of assets presents an entirely different picture, in part because U.S. investments abroad were made many years ago and have since increased greatly in value. Foreign investments in the United States have been made more recently and have not increased so much in value.

The problem was particularly acute with regard to "direct investment," the ownership of plants or oil wells or companies in other countries. Direct investment by Americans abroad, to a considerable extent made in an earlier era, has jumped enormously in value. I use two techniques[15] to try to get a measure of the current value of this investment. One entails adjusting on the basis of changes in stock market values in various countries. The other involves an adjustment on the basis of product price indices to obtain estimates of "replacement cost" or "current cost," as the BEA does in its national income and product accounts.[16] For 1989 we estimated that, for a book value of U.S. direct investment in the rest of the world of $373 billion, the market value was $889 billion and the replacement cost was $801 billion. The undercount was on the order of half a trillion dollars!

Other adjustments were in order. The official accounts were carrying the gold owned by the Treasury as an American "asset," presumably because it was equivalent to U.S. Treasury or Federal Reserve holdings of reserves in the form of foreign currencies. This gold was valued at its nominal value of $42.22 per ounce. Bringing gold up to market value added about another $95 billion to our "international investment

---

[15] In work with Paul J. Pieper. See "The World's Greatest Debtor Nation?" *The North American Review of Economics and Finance*, vol. 1, no. 1, 1990, pp. 9–32.
[16] This entails estimating what it would cost, at current market prices, to replace existing structures and equipment.

position." With corrections and adjustments we wiped out the bulk of the U.S. "debt"—virtually all in 1987, about 80 percent in 1988, and about two-thirds in 1989.[17] The figures for 1988 and 1989 are shown in Table 4.2.

There are even further corrections. A potentially important one would be the inclusion of the assets of new U.S. permanent residents or immigrants as part of our investment position.[18] Some of them are wealthy and when they settle in the United States their wealth, whether in their countries of origin or in Swiss bank accounts, becomes our wealth.

Responding to professional criticism,[19] the Bureau of Economic Analysis stopped publishing the bottom line of the international investment position. It explained that its summary of claims involved "adding apples and oranges" in a mixture of original cost and current value accounting, and that further work was necessary to prepare consistent sets of accounts. When this work was completed, the BEA began publishing new measures that offered alternate adjustments to market value and replacement costs. The BEA adjustments were somewhat less than ours but did knock three or four hundred billion dollars from the alleged "debt" of the nation. Perhaps for that reason, the politicians did not focus heavily in the 1992 electoral struggle on our status as "the world's greatest debtor nation," although by any measure, the international investment position of the United States appeared to be turning more negative.

---

[17] Taken from Robert Eisner and Paul J. Pieper, "Real Foreign Investment in Perspective," *The Annals of the American Academy of Political and Social Science,* July 1991, Table 2, p. 25.

[18] The BEA measures of national income, assets, and liabilities are all defined to apply to residents of the United States, citizens or not, who have been here twelve months or more. Foreign holdings of new residents of the United States should become assets of the United States and their assets in the United States should cease being liabilities to the rest of the world. In practice, these corrections are rarely made.

[19] Particularly by Eisner and Pieper in "The World's Greatest Debtor Nation?," presented at American Economic Association meetings in 1988, and by Michael Ulan and William G. Dewald, "The U.S. Net International Investment Position," in James A. Dorn and William A. Niskanen, eds., *Dollars, Deficits and Trade* (Boston: Kluwer Academic Publishers, 1989).

Table 4.2 *U.S. Net Direct Investment Position and Net International Investment Position*
(billions of dollars)

	Book Value	Market Value	Replacement Value
A. U.S. Net Direct Investment Position, 1989			
U.S. Direct Investment Abroad	373.4	888.6	800.7
Foreign Direct Investment in the U.S.	400.8	544.1	452.9
Net Direct Investment Position	−27.4	344.6	347.8
		1988	1989
B. U.S. Net International Investment Position			
Official Net International Investment Position		−533.1*	−663.7*
Adjustment for Direct Investment			
Replacement Cost		376.3	375.2
Market Value		358.9	371.9
Adjustment for Third World Loans		−42.7	−38.9
Adjustment for Gold		96.4	94.6
Adjusted U.S. Net International Investment Position			
Replacement Cost		−101.1	−236.1
Market Value		−118.5	−232.8

*As totalled by authors in conformity with old (abandoned) BEA methodology. From Eisner and Pieper, "Real Foreign Investment in Perspective," pp. 22–35.

The issue does involve, however, more than devising correct and relevant measures. If we keep importing more than we export or, more precisely, show negative net foreign investment, there are economic consequences. What are they? Can the economy react fairly automatically and painlessly to them? Are there policy actions to be taken?

WHAT ARE THE CONSEQUENCES OF FOREIGN INVESTMENT AND WHAT IS TO BE DONE?

In 1988, at perhaps the height of the "debtor nation" furor, the U.S. balance on current account was reported as minus $163 billion.[20] Assuming the figure was correct, that meant that foreigners invested $163 billion more in the United States than we invested abroad. If this were repeated, year after year, would not our children and grandchildren bear the burden? At that rate, in six years foreigners would be receiving from us the return on a trillion dollars of accumulated net investment in the United States.

That worst-case scenario, which was not in fact realized, was widely bemoaned. Yet what would even that have amounted to? At a real rate of interest (nominal rate minus the rate of inflation), or real rate of return, of 4 percent, which may be extravagant, that would come to $40 billion per year. By 1994, we shall have a gross domestic product in the neighborhood of $6.8 trillion.[21] The $40 billion we might pay to foreigners would come to near six-tenths of 1 percent of our GDP, not insignificant but hardly the stuff of national disaster. By contrast, one percentage point of unemployment, with all its concomitant losses, is estimated to cost us some 2 percent of GDP. Reducing the unemployment rate by just 0.3 percent would give us the extra output and earnings to pay our foreign investors.

---

[20] According to most recent BEA estimates, the current account deficit peaked in 1987 at $167.3 billion.
[21] According to estimates by the WEFA Group in the fall of 1993.

Another response to those who worry about foreigners taking over the nation is a reminder of the value of our total national wealth. The tangible or physical wealth alone comes to some $25 trillion. A more relevant figure might include the present value of the prospective earnings of those currently in the workforce.[22] Discounted at that same 4 percent rate of return, that would be well over $100 trillion. Even in the worst-case scenario, a trillion dollar increase in foreign claims on the wealth of those now working would have come to less than one percent of that wealth.

There is further comfort available for those debt gloom-and-doomers who will accept it. The cost to the United States of foreign ownership of our wealth, as I have pointed out, is the income on that wealth we pay to foreigners. The latest, corrected BEA figures on the international investment position of the United States show us at a negative $521.3 billion on a current-cost basis and a negative $611.5 billion on a market value basis. If foreigners have $500 billion or $600 billion more invested with us than we have invested with them, we should expect them to be earning more in the United States than we are earning on our investments in their countries. But what are the actual figures on net investment income in our international accounts? As late as 1992 they were still in the black. Net investment income totalled $6 billion

---

[22]The present value of an amount at some future date is the amount today that would be equivalent, taking into account the interest or other return that could be had by lending or investing that amount today. Thus, if the rate of interest or return is 4 percent, the present value of $104 one year from now is $100, since $100 today could be lent or invested at 4 percent and return a total of $104 one year from today. We can write, $100 = $104/1.04, $96.15 = $100/1.04, $100 = $108.16/(1.04)^2$, $92.46 = $100/(1.04)^2$ or, generally, $PV = X_t/(1 + i)^t$, for an amount t years from now.

Still more generally, when we are dealing with the present value of a stream of future returns, the present value of that stream, actually the sum of the present values of each element in the stream, may be written, $PV = \Sigma X_t/(1 + i)^t$, for every year, t, X is not zero. On the assumption that i is positive (and the simplifying assumption that it is the same for all years), even an infinite stream will have a finite present value. If the amount, X, were the same in every year, for example, the present value of an infinite stream of X, for example, a permanent income of X for all future years, would be $X*(1 + i)/i$. For a value of i equal to 4 percent, or .04, this would come to $X*1.04/.04$ or 26 times X.

for the year, and turned only trivially negative in 1993. Receipts from U.S. assets abroad were estimated by the BEA at $110.6 billion in 1992, while our payments on foreign assets in the United States were put at only $104.4 billion.

Some suggest that these numbers stem from higher rates of return that Americans enjoy on more risky investments in the rest of the world. Our rates of return on direct investment abroad, in particular, appear considerably higher than foreign rates of return on direct investment in the United States. Another possibility, though, is that the official accounts are still understating the value of U.S. direct investment abroad, and hence overstating their rates of return and understating our net international investment position. We might then not be a "debtor nation" at all. The correct, market value of U.S. investments in (claims on) the rest of the world may be greater than the market value of claims of foreigners on the United States. The bottom line, in any event, is whether we are paying foreigners more than they are paying us, and until at least the last year we have not been.

A funny thing happened after 1987. That huge deficit of $167.3 billion on current account came down sharply, to $127.2 billion in 1988, to $101.6 billion in 1989, to $91.9 billion in 1990, and to $8.3 billion in 1991, before rising to $66.4 billion in 1992. That result coincided, by the way, with sharply mounting *budget* deficits after 1989. In part, the results can be attributed to the usual, lagged response of our exports and imports to the drastic fall in the real value—and cost—of the dollar in foreign exchange.[23] That fall was from

---

[23] This lagged response is described as a J-curve. If we plot the current account balance on the vertical axis and time on the horizontal axis, we frequently find that in response to a fall in the value of a nation's currency its current account balance first falls and then rises, surpassing its original level only after two or three years. This is plausibly attributed to the slowness of old and possible new exporters taking advantage of new market potential and the slowness of people and business in changing their purchasing habits in the light of higher prices for imported goods. Thus, for the United States for example, a fall in the value of the dollar might bring little initial increase in exports but possibly even a significant *increase* in the dollar value of imports as Americans at first keep buying the same number of Toyotas and Mercedeses even though their prices have risen.

a trade-weighted index of 132 in 1985 to 91 by 1987 and subsequently to a range in the 80s. When our goods get cheaper, foreigners do buy more of them.

THE RECESSION CURE

The fall in the current account deficit to virtually zero in 1991 must also be traced to the substantial recession in the American economy.[24] We can indeed "cure" our trade deficit problems if we can create enough unemployment and hard times at home. Americans who are too poor to buy American goods also reduce their purchases of goods from abroad. The relapse to a current account deficit of $66 billion in 1992 (net foreign investment of $-$55 billion in the slightly different national income and product accounts) can be attributed largely to a recession in much of the rest of the world. (They may have "caught" the recession from the United States.) Demand for our exports was curbed, matching the curb in our demand for theirs.

There are some important lessons here. First, a current account deficit—and hence negative net foreign investment—may be a result of relative prosperity. One should not try to eliminate or reduce that deficit by eliminating the prosperity. It is widely argued, as I will note below, that budget deficits contribute to current account deficits—to negative net foreign investment or "borrowing" from abroad. The way to reduce foreign borrowing, we are told, is to reduce our domestic borrowing, that is, reduce the federal budget deficit. This has a certain plausibility and is in a sense—although a perverse sense—correct.

As noted, the current account deficit almost disappeared in 1991 when the budget deficit soared. So how can *reducing* the budget deficit reduce the foreign deficit? There is a good

---

[24] And to the payments by foreign governments to the United States for the war against Iraq. Our military services turned out to be a major export!

explanation. The budget deficit increase in 1991 was a cyclical increase linked with the slump in the economy, a slump deepened if not brought on, I might add, by the reduction in the underlying *structural* deficit in the 1990 budget deal between President Bush and the Congress. What we must look for are the effects of changes in that structural deficit, that is, changes independent of cyclical changes in the economy. The structural deficit is thus reduced by tax increases and spending cuts such as those envisaged in the 1990 Bush–Congress deal and in the Clinton program advanced in 1993. The slowdown in the economy these policies may cause may increase the actual total deficit, which may be seen to be the sum of its structural and cyclical components.

Reductions in the structural deficit may well reduce the trade and current account deficits. As we have less to spend we buy less at home and less in the rest of the world as well. As we buy less from foreigners we give up less of our currency to foreigners in payment for their goods and services. The reductions in the structural budget deficit thus reduce our borrowing from abroad—the increase in foreign holdings of dollars or investments in the United States—precisely to the extent they slow the U.S. economy. There ought to be a better way, and there is.

A BETTER WAY

That better way is to allow exchange rates to respond to market forces. This does not mean that the Federal Reserve should intervene in foreign exchange markets and force the dollar down. But it certainly should not stand in the way by keeping interest rates high, thus putting the dollar in great demand by international investors, here and in the rest of the world. And the Fed might help by judiciously reminding the Japanese, as did Secretary of the Treasury Lloyd Bentsen early in 1993, and other foreign bankers and governments where appropriate, that putting higher values on *their* currencies might be a good idea. This should encourage them to keep their own economies strong and to avoid exchange intervention to keep their currencies weak.

In free markets, we would expect current account deficits ultimately to be self-correcting. At some point foreigners will have accumulated as much in the way of dollar assets as they are comfortable with. If we then had continued current account deficits, giving them more dollars, they would try to exchange these dollars for their own currencies.

Where will a Japanese looking for yen find them? With another Japanese! How could they be persuaded to give up yen for dollars? The same way people wishing to sell stocks get someone to buy them: accepting whatever price they can get. Japanese deciding not to accumulate dollars, let alone *de*cumulate or "pull out" of their dollar investments, do so by finding others with yen—or any other foreign currency they may be willing to hold—to accept the dollars. The efforts to sell dollars drive down their price, as efforts to sell stocks drive down their prices. But just as a "wave of selling" leaves the same total holdings of stock, but at lower values, a wave of foreign selling of dollars leaves the same quantity of dollars in foreign hands, but at lower values in terms of foreign currencies.

The foreign accumulation of dollars—and hence of dollar investment—will end only when its mirror image, the U.S. current account deficit, disappears. As the dollar depreciates, this may occur as our exports, sufficiently cheap to foreigners, increase and their exports, sufficiently expensive to us, decline.[25]

To some extent, then, we may expect self-correcting forces. If foreigners feel they are accumulating more than they want

---

[25] It should be recognized that though the export boom and cut in imports brought on by a cheaper dollar will add to jobs and gross domestic product in a less-than-full-employment economy, it will also entail a "terms-of-trade effect" that will leave us worse off. We will find that we are having to give more of our domestic production in trade for any given amount of imports from abroad. What the Bureau of Economic Analysis calls the "gross domestic product on a command basis" will not rise as much as the usual measure of real GDP. If we are close to full employment, so that GDP by its usual measure cannot rise much, the GDP on a command basis may actually decline, and with it our living standards.

in U.S. investments, they will try to sell dollars for other currencies—usually their own—and drive down the value and cost of the dollar until the changing trade balance sufficiently slows or ends that dollar accumulation. There is another possible scenario. Foreigners may *want* to accumulate dollars.

With all our problems, we remain arguably the most stable and prosperous nation in the world. As foreigners also grow more prosperous, their wealth grows with their incomes. With good financial prudence, they may wish to have mixed portfolios, keeping some of their investments in the safe and stable United States. They move their portfolios into American investments by acquiring dollars, and as they try to acquire dollars they drive up the price of dollars. They can then get dollars in the aggregate either by running a current account surplus—our current account deficit—or by persuading us to buy their assets. They drive up the value of the dollar sufficiently to give us an "unfavorable" trade balance—and give themselves a surplus—or make their assets so cheap that we buy more of them.

We may then find ourselves in a situation where we are acting as a safe bank for the rest of the world. We offer foreigners investments at lower returns, selling them the safety and stability of assets in a prosperous economy. This might also explain our recent positive balances in net investment income even though, if the figures are to be believed, foreigners' investments in the United States have been worth more than our investments in the rest of the world. Not a bad deal after all! We get the benefit of the foreign investment without having to pay for it!

IS THE UNITED STATES BEGGARING THE REST
OF THE WORLD?

International do-gooders have one final complaint about the United States. They bemoan the fact that by running large budget deficits, which presumably created the

trade and current account deficits and associated negative net
foreign investment, the United States is draining the rest of
the world of capital that other countries need far more than
we do.

One simple counterargument is that if the rest of the world
chooses to invest in the United States rather than elsewhere,
it is because it finds U.S. investment more desirable. As I
have pointed out, net investment in the United States could
not occur without U.S. current account deficits. They are created in part, as we shall see in later chapters, by the domestic
prosperity that structural budget deficits seem to foster. They
are also created by high values of the dollar, which may themselves be brought on by the demand for dollars precisely because, taking into account the frequently lesser risks, investment in the United States appears more profitable than
investment elsewhere.

But suppose investment is attracted to the United States
because the return on the dollar is raised by high domestic
interest rates maintained by U.S. monetary authorities. Foreigners—and Americans—may then have a more legitimate
complaint. They do not seem frequently though to have registered it. They have rather, most conspicuously in the case of
Germany, and France and the United Kingdom too, kept their
own interest rates too high, slowing their own economies and
so curbing the demand for U.S. exports that would right the
international balances.

There is, however, a most important other side of the coin
of the negative foreign investment registered by the United
States in much of the past decade. It is the U.S. import surpluses, which have fueled foreign business around the world.
Have the U.S. budget deficits injured foreign economies by
causing negative net foreign investment by the United States,
which drained capital from the rest of the world? I have found,
to the contrary,[26] that structural, inflation-adjusted budget

---

[26] Again in work with Paul J. Pieper, particularly, "Measurement and Effects of
Government Debt and Deficits," in *Economic Policy and National Accounting in Inflationary Conditions, Studies in Banking and Finance*, no. 2, 1986, North Holland,

deficits in the United States were associated with greater economic growth over the years 1971 to 1982 in six major trading partners in the OECD (Canada, France, the former West Germany, Italy, Japan, and the United Kingdom). It would appear that any consumption binges promoted by U.S. budget deficits, to the extent that they brought on import surpluses which drained those foreign countries of capital, left our trading partners crying all the way to their (American) banks.

It may still be argued that U.S. import surpluses did not always spill over to less developed countries. These less developed countries were deprived of the foreign capital, invested in the United States, which could have been used to fuel their growth. Remedies might then be in order. It would appear, however, that more appropriate action to help these less developed countries is possible than U.S. moves to fiscal austerity or interference with free trade. This action might include: ending the scandalous expenditure by many of these nations for often suicidal armaments; easing of criteria set by the International Monetary Fund and the World Bank, which frequently impose such fiscal and monetary austerity as to destroy possibilities of economic growth; opening U.S. borders to a full range of unrestricted imports from less developed countries; and judicious international aid programs to encourage investment in human and physical capital.

The United States has the largest and strongest economy in the world. It can best help itself and others by pursuing policies—those I have been and will be enunciating—focused on making that economy, in cooperation with the rest of the world, larger and stronger still.

---

and in a French version, "Dette et déficit gouvernementaux: mesures et effets," in *Annales d'Économie et de Statistique*, no. 3, 1986.

CHAPTER 5

Sense and Nonsense about Budget Deficits

"If the Treasury were to fill old bottles with bank-notes, bury them at suitable depths in disused coal-mines which were then filled to the surface with town rubbish, and leave it to private enterprise on well-tried principles of *laissez-faire* to dig the notes up again (the right to do so being obtained, of course, by tendering for leases of the note-bearing territory), there need be no more unemployment and, with the help of the repercussions, the real income of the community, and its capital wealth also, would probably become a great deal greater than it actually is. It would indeed be more sensible to build houses and the like; but if there are political and practical difficulties in the way of this, the above would be better than nothing."—John Maynard Keynes, *The General Theory of Employment, Interest and Money* (New York: Harcourt, Brace and Company, 1936), p. 129.

"Balancing the budget will always remain a goal of any administration. . . . That does not mean to say that you can pick a specific date and say, 'Here, all things must give way before a balanced budget.' It is a question of where the importance of a balanced budget comes in; but it must be the aim of any sound money program. . . . When it becomes clear that the Government has to step in, as far as I'm concerned, the full power of Government, of Government credit, and of everything the Government has will move in to see that there is no widespread unemployment and we never again have a repetition of conditions that so

many of you here remember when we had unemployment."—Dwight Eisenhower in 1953.[1]

Almost everybody talks about budget deficits. Almost
everybody seems in principle to be against them. And almost
no one, literally, knows what he is talking about.

Maybe it goes back to something deep in Calvinist tradi-
tion, that we must suffer rather than borrow. "No gain without pain," we are told. We must pay higher taxes now, or
forego useful or desirable government spending now, to be
better off in the future—in the next world?

Perhaps it has new, more recent political roots. Republicans
have been attacking Democrats over deficits since the New
Deal of Franklin D. Roosevelt. He pledged to "balance the
budget," but never succeeded. Then, with the huge Reagan-
era deficits, Democrats thought they had their chance and
they attacked Republicans on the issue. In his independent course, Ross Perot now makes a big deal of "the
deficit"—instead of applying his wealth to reduce it—and ad-
vances extreme "solutions" including a "balanced-budget"
amendment to the Constitution. And President Clinton, in
his critical initial State of the Union address on the economy,
was constrained to present a comprehensive deficit reduction
package.

The public has always seemed to agree in wide proportions
that the deficit should be eliminated. But it is far from clear
that any candidates—Republicans, Democrats, or Perot—
have ever won an election on the deficit. Many, by opposing
popular deficit-increasing measures or by supporting tax increases to reduce it, have lost. With all the hoopla about deficit reduction, recall those results of the Gallup Poll reported
at the time of that State of the Union address. Asked, "Which
is more important, creating jobs or reducing the deficit?," 65

---

[1] From Herbert Stein, *The Fiscal Revolution in America* (Chicago: University of Chicago Press, 1969), pp. 298–299. Quoted in James D. Savage, *Balanced Budgets and
American Politics* (Ithaca and London: Cornell University Press, 1988), pp. 174–175.

percent of respondents chose "creating jobs" and only 28 percent "reducing the deficit." And a poll among Perot voters conducted in April 1993 for the Democratic Leadership Council (the centrist group of which Governor Clinton had been chairman) "challenged the conventional wisdom that reducing the deficit was the overriding concern of Perot voters. It found that only one-fourth of them cited the deficit as the first or second most important problem facing the country. Far more gave higher priority to the economy, jobs and health care."[2]

WHAT IS THE DEFICIT AND HOW IS IT MEASURED?

Few have any notion how the deficit is measured. Many, including the major TV news anchorpeople, editorial writers, journalists in leading newspapers, even including the *New York Times,* and countless politicians, confuse the deficit and the debt. The deficit is the amount by which expenditures exceed tax revenues in a given period and hence the amount that must be borrowed or added to the debt over that period. The debt is the amount owed at any point in time, what has been borrowed and not paid back, or the sum of all previous net borrowings.

President Clinton himself, in his inaugural address, succumbed to the public looseness of phrase, if not general confusion, in saying that we must "cut our massive debt." If he meant the federal debt, that in fact is quite beyond reasonable possibility in the foreseeable future. Recently, Clinton has more realistically talked of cutting the *deficit* by $145 billion as against forecasts of what it will be in 1997. But that would still leave a deficit of some $160 billion and the debt hence *growing* by that amount annually. Only a *surplus* would reduce the debt.

---

[2]*New York Times,* July 8, 1993, p. A4.

Yet we still hear the president and others talking about reducing the debt. Witness a pious Mobil advertisement (*Newsweek*, February 8, 1993) which argues, "Clearly, one of President Clinton's and the 103rd Congress's primary tasks must be to reduce the federal debt to the extent practical as soon as possible," adding inexplicably the internally redundant clause, "and to balance the budget to prevent further deficits."

Many do not understand the measures of the debt about which they speak so much. The most frequently cited figure, approaching $4.4 trillion at the end of the 1993 fiscal year, is a gross "total," which includes over $1 trillion of "debt" held within the government, largely by trust funds such as those for social security for old age and retirement. But a more meaningful figure, relevant to household spending, financial markets, and business decisions, and excluding accounting transactions between one arm of government and another, is for the "gross federal debt held by the public." This is more like $3.3 trillion dollars. And that figure might be reduced by some $300 billion for the Treasury securities held by the Federal Reserve banks; since these are technically public corporations, their holdings are included in the debt held by the public. That leaves the federal government with a relevant debt of just about $3 trillion.

We have a vast number of measures of the federal deficit, but most of the official ones should horrify any private or public accountant concerned with applying sensible accounting principles. Aside from differences between the Bureau of Economic Analysis national income accounts and the OMB and congressional budgets, differences between budgets with and without "deposit insurance" outlays (chiefly for the savings and loan bailout), distinctions among basic, baseline, and structural deficits, and the bewildering proclivity of the Congress to place vast expenditures and receipts "off-budget," U.S. federal practice violates a basic principle of accounting followed by private business, most state and local governments in the United States, and national governments over the entire world: it does not distinguish between current or operating outlays and capital expenditures.

That makes as much sense, as I pointed out earlier, as it would for a family not to distinguish between borrowing to finance the purchase of a new home or invest in the children's education and borrowing to finance gambling losses at Las Vegas. If there were no separate capital accounts, almost every large corporation in the United States would be reporting "deficits" or losses. Of course, private business excludes capital outlays from its current account and charges only depreciation in presenting its income or profit and loss statements. And many state and local governments in the United States are required in their constitutions to balance current or operating budgets, while capital outlays, as for roads and bridges and new water systems or school buildings, are financed by borrowing.

Private business currently capitalizes only tangible or physical investment in plant and equipment, not intangible investment such as R&D expenditures. It thus excludes current tangible capital expenditures for plant and equipment from its current account but does include depreciation charges on its capital stock, that is, on past investment. In a growing firm, current investment is virtually always greater than depreciation, which is an average of past investment. Including depreciation rather than current investment thus permits private business income statements of profitable firms to retain a bottom line in the black.

Assume, counterfactually, that federal accounting conformed to private business practice and tangible capital investment was excluded but the depreciation on past tangible investment was included in the budget. The resulting U.S. federal budget deficit on current account, however, would at this time be little, or not at all, less than the overall deficits generally reported. This reflects a situation of which we should be much more aware, virtually zero net public investment in physical infrastructure. Our public physical plant is wearing out at least as fast as it is being replaced. With a more comprehensive measure of investment, though, including the Office of Management and Budget's estimates of "Major Federal Capital Outlays" for research and development and education and training as well as physical capital, net investment, reflecting (however inadequately) the needs of our growing population, would be positive. Its exclusion would have reduced the measure of the deficit by perhaps $80 billion of the $255 billion reported for the 1993 fiscal year.

Given some $180 billion per year of federal grants to state and local governments, it might make some sense to present a consolidated account for all of government, as the Bureau of Economic Analysis does in its national income and product accounts. If we do that and then separate out all capital expenditures for both tangible and intangible investment, we find that while the total consolidated budget remains in deficit in 1992, to the amount of $269 billion, as was shown in Table 3.2, the current account portion of that deficit is only $97 billion.

A large part of the deficit is accountable directly to our slow economy and high unemployment. The Congressional Budget Office indeed estimates that each percentage point of unemployment adds, in the short term, $50 billion to the deficit, with the amount growing over time as additional deficit adds more to debt and subsequent interest payments.

By those estimates, if unemployment in 1993 were back at the 5.0 percent level it attained in March 1989 at the beginning of the Bush administration, the deficit would be $100 billion less. By 1996, as a consequence of interest payment savings on a lesser accumulated debt and a larger economy, the 2 percentage point reduction in unemployment from what it was in June 1993 would make the deficit some $130 billion less. Virtually all of the Clinton–Gore commitment to deficit reduction could be realized by that minimal reduction in unemployment. Achieving the 4 percent rate that has long been our target, or a 3 percent rate such as we had during the Vietnam War, could bring an even greater reduction in the deficit.

THE DEFICIT IN A GROWING ECONOMY

In a growing economy with a growing population almost everything grows—births and deaths, marriages and divorces, borrowing and repayment, as well as income, wealth, assets, and debt. The government's criterion for increasing debt—for determining how much borrowing there should be—should relate to income, as with prudent private borrowers, banks, and businesses. People should not owe more than is warranted by their income. They should not indefinitely let their debt grow faster than their income.

One may well argue that a responsible deficit target, similar to responsible targets for private business and households, is that debt over the long run grow no faster than income or, for the nation, gross domestic product. At the end of the 1939 fiscal year the gross federal debt held by the public came to $41 billion, 47 percent of GDP, as shown in Table 5.1. In 1946, after World War II, it reached $242 billion, or 114 percent of GDP. By 1980, with deficits in all the years from 1961 on, the debt had grown in absolute amount to $709 billion, but had fallen, relatively, to 27 percent of GDP. At the end of the 1993 fiscal year the debt held by the public was $3,247 billion, almost 52 percent of GDP, but still little more than its proportion of 47 percent over half a century earlier, as the New Deal was giving way to World War II. And it was less than half of its proportion just after that war. We may note both the short period changes and the secular swings of the debt/GDP ratio in Table 5.1 and Figure 5.1.

There is nothing sacrosanct about any particular debt/GDP ratio. In periods of recession we may expect deficits to rise and the debt to grow more rapidly than GDP, which will itself be growing much less rapidly, if at all. The debt/GDP ratio then should almost certainly rise. If there is need for major investment, debt may again grow faster than GDP.

But suppose we were to keep the debt/GDP ratio constant. It is instructive to note what this "equilibrium" target would imply for our current situation, as shown below:

Deficit with Constant Debt/GDP Ratio, Projected Deficit
and Deficit with Two Percentage Points Less Unemployment

	Debt	GDP	Ratio
1992 (approximate)	$3,000b	$6,000b	0.5
6% Growth	180b	360b	0.5
1993	$3,180b	$6,360b	0.5

Deficit = Increase in Debt = $180 billion

Final Bush–OMB projected 1993 deficit:	$327 billion
Actual 1993 deficit reported in October 1993	$255 billion
Deficit with 2% less unemployment:	$155 billion
Deficit with 2% less unemployment and 1% lower interest rates	$125 billion
Deficit to maintain constant debt/GDP ratio	$180 billion

Table 5.1   *Debt, GDP, Debt/GDP Ratio, and Change in Debt/GDP Ratio, 1939–1993*

Year	Debt	GDP	Debt/GDP Ratio	Change in Debt/GDP Ratio
	(billions of dollars)			(percent)
1939	41.4	87.9	47.1	—
1940	42.8	95.4	44.9	−2.3
1941	48.2	112.5	42.8	−2.0
1942	67.8	141.8	47.8	5.0
1943	127.8	175.4	72.8	25.0
1944	184.8	201.7	91.6	18.8
1945	235.2	212.1	110.9	19.3
1946	241.9	212.5	113.8	2.9
1947	224.3	223.1	100.5	−13.3
1948	216.3	247.3	87.5	−13.1
1949	214.3	259.8	82.5	−5.0
1950	219.0	273.1	80.2	−2.3
1951	214.3	309.3	69.3	−10.9
1952	214.8	340.7	63.1	−6.2
1953	218.4	359.9	60.7	−2.4
1954	224.5	370.5	60.6	−0.1
1955	226.6	387.6	58.5	−2.1
1956	222.2	415.3	53.5	−5.0
1957	219.3	437.4	50.1	−3.4
1958	226.3	451.7	50.1	0.0
1959	234.7	474.5	49.5	−0.6

Table 5.1   (Continued)

Year	Debt	GDP	Debt/GDP Ratio	Change in Debt/GDP Ratio
	(billions of dollars)			(percent)
1960	236.8	503.8	47.0	−2.5
1961	238.4	522.5	45.6	−1.4
1962	248.0	551.7	45.0	−0.7
1963	254.0	587.3	43.2	−1.7
1964	256.8	625.5	41.1	−2.2
1965	260.8	675.3	38.6	−2.4
1966	263.7	736.3	35.8	−2.8
1967	266.6	792.0	33.7	−2.2
1968	289.5	851.8	34.0	0.3
1969	278.1	924.4	30.1	−3.9
1970	283.2	985.1	28.7	−1.3
1971	303.0	1,053.9	28.7	0.0
1972	322.4	1,152.1	28.0	−0.8
1973	340.9	1,278.3	26.7	−1.3
1974	343.7	1,404.1	24.5	−2.2
1975	394.7	1,522.3	25.9	1.5
1976	477.4	1,677.2	28.5	2.5
1977	549.1	1,922.7	28.6	0.1
1978	607.1	2,168.1	28.0	−0.6
1979	639.8	2,424.6	26.4	−1.6
1980	709.3	2,653.1	26.7	0.3
1981	784.8	2,950.0	26.6	−0.1
1982	919.2	3,119.9	29.5	2.9
1983	1,131.0	3,341.1	33.9	4.4
1984	1,300.0	3,684.1	35.3	1.4
1985	1,499.4	3,973.3	37.7	2.5
1986	1,736.2	4,211.1	41.2	3.5
1987	1,888.1	4,472.1	42.2	1.0
1988	2,050.3	4,810.3	42.6	0.4
1989	2,189.3	5,163.2	42.4	−0.2
1990	2,410.4	5,472.3	44.0	1.6
1991	2,687.9	5,678.7	47.3	3.3
1992	2,998.6	5,959.6	50.3	3.0
1993	3,247.2	6,295.0	51.6	1.3

Sources: Debt figures from *Economic Report of the President,* 1993, Table B-74, p. 435. Debt is "gross federal debt (end of period) held by the public" (1993 figure from Monthly Treasury Statement, October 28, 1993, Table 6, "total borrowing from the public"). Gross domestic product is a weighted average reflecting the varying ends of fiscal years, June 30 until 1976 and September 30 thereafter, calculated from GDP series in *Survey of Current Business,* September 1993, Table 1, p. 47, and, for 1993, Bureau of Economic Analysis release BEA 93-49, October 28, 1993.

Figure 5.1 *Debt/GDP Ratio and Changes in Debt/GDP Ratio,*
1939–1993

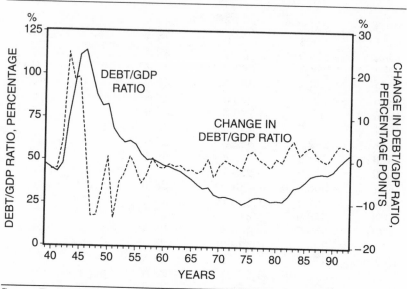

Source: *Economic Report of the President,* 1993, Table B-74, p. 435.

The Bush Office of Management and Budget's final deficit projections were based on the "Blue Chip" private forecasters' anticipations of an unemployment rate averaging 7.2 percent for all of calendar year 1993! Greeted with much expression of concern, the projections had a mismeasured deficit declining from $327 billion in 1993 to $270 billion in 1994 and $230 billion in 1995 before beginning to rise again to $266 billion in 1996, $305 billion in 1997, and $320 billion in 1998. They assumed unemployment above 6 percent through 1995 and still at 5.7 percent in 1998. They also assumed 91-day Treasury bills rising, unaccountably, from their current rates under 3 percent to over 5 percent, thus adding perhaps another $50 billion to the annual deficit.

Those projections, though, even if correct, would have had the deficit/GDP ratio below 3.9 percent and the debt/GDP ratio virtually stable, at 57 percent, by 1998. The debt would then be growing at a 6.67 percent per annum rate, with a projected GDP growth of 5.93 percent. If the rate of GDP growth were over 6.67 percent, the debt/GDP ratio would be declining. If unemployment were down only to its 5.2 percent rate of 1989 and Treasury bill rates were still around 3 percent, the resulting 1997 deficit would be not $305 billion but on the order of $200 billion, or 2.5 percent of GDP. With a slightly more ambitious 7 percent rate of growth of GDP, the debt/GDP ratio would then be headed for an equilibrium ratio of 36 percent, well below its current figure of slightly over 50 percent.[3] In a meaningful, relative sense, President Clinton would have reduced "our massive debt."

HOW DO DEFICITS HURT?—OR DO THEY?

Much of what is written and said about the damage done by federal budget deficits is sheer nonsense, no matter how often repeated. First, of course, the notion that the federal government will go bankrupt because it is unable to pay

---

[3] Here, the lesson of a little bit of elementary algebra is striking. The differential for the change in the debt/GDP ratio, B/Y, is

$$\Delta(B/Y) = (Y\Delta B - B\Delta Y)/Y^2 = \Delta B/Y - (B/Y)(\Delta Y/Y).$$

For the debt/GDP ratio, B/Y, to stay the same, the debt must grow at the same rate as GDP, or $\Delta B/B = \Delta Y/Y$; substituting $\Delta B/B$ for $\Delta Y/Y$ sets the equation to zero. But the deficit equals the change in the debt, or $D = \Delta B$. More generally, then,

$$\Delta(B/Y) \gtreqless 0 \text{ as } D/Y \gtreqless (B/Y)(\Delta Y/Y);$$

the debt/GDP ratio increases, decreases, or stays the same as the deficit ratio is greater than, less than, or equal to the product of the debt ratio and the rate of growth of GDP.

For a constant debt–GDP ratio we have

$$\Delta(B/Y) = D/Y - (B/Y)(\Delta Y/Y) = 0, \text{ whence}$$
$$B/Y = D/Y \div \Delta Y/Y;$$

the equilibrium or "balanced" debt/GDP ratio equals the deficit/GDP ratio divided by the rate of growth of GDP. A permanently higher deficit ratio will not raise the debt/GDP ratio indefinitely; it will only raise it to a new, higher equilibrium. And a higher rate of growth of GDP will lower the equilibrium debt/GDP ratio. Thus, even if the 1993 deficit/GDP ratio of 4 percent were not reduced, if the rate of growth of GDP were permanently 6 percent, the debt/GDP ratio would eventually rise, from its current 52 percent, to 67 percent, but go no higher.

off or service its debt is absurd. A sovereign government need never overtly repudiate a debt in its own currency. It can always tax those subject to its laws, including bond holders, to get the necessary proceeds. Or, as I pointed out earlier, it can simply print the money needed—in the case of the United States, have the Federal Reserve buy Treasury securities. That may have other consequences; under some circumstances, although clearly not all, it may add to inflation.[4] But in any event, there is no issue of bankruptcy for debt in dollars.[5] The debt may be repaid in cheaper dollars but there is no reason why it cannot be repaid.

"SPENDING OUR CHILDREN'S MONEY"

Ross Perot has warned repeatedly that we are "spending our children's money." But our children's money has not yet been printed and will of course be printed or supplied when our children need it, in whatever quantities the interaction of the monetary authorities and our banking and financial system then determine. Alan Greenspan's successors in the Federal Reserve will always be able to supply money for our children. What they cannot supply and what, we shall see, may be lacking, are the real resources of capital, public and private, tangible and intangible, human and nonhuman, with which we now fail to endow our children.

We are also told that our continuing deficits mean we are passing ever greater debt on to our children. This is literally true. Our children will be the *owners* of all those Treasury bills, notes, and bonds that constitute the debt. That will give them a nice cushion of accumulated savings. Is that necessarily so bad?

We are further told that the interest burden of the debt,

---

[4]Monetizing the debt—presumably by having the Federal Reserve buy up interest-bearing securities—adds the further stimulus of liquidity and lower real interest rates, as discussed in Chapter 7.
[5]Debt denominated in a foreign currency, which is not the case for the United States, is quite another matter.

currently about $180 billion per year, is a heavy drag on the economy. In fact it comes to less than 3 percent of GDP. But, more fundamentally, the interest payments of the Treasury are, after all, income to their recipients. Any taxes that may be levied to finance the payments are then matched by added income.

It is sometimes argued that this involves a regressive redistribution of income, on the assumption that the rich receive interest income financed by taxes paid by the poor. A moment's reflection casts major doubt on that assumption. The ultimate beneficiaries of the interest receipts—via pension funds, insurance, and banking services as well as savings bonds—must be mainly in the large middle class. And relatively little is paid in taxes by the very poor. The social cost of debt and deficits will have to be found elsewhere.

On a more sophisticated level, it might be argued that if marginal tax rates—the percent of each additional dollar of income that goes for taxes—are 3 percentage points higher to finance interest payments, work effort may be discouraged. People receiving large proportions of their income in the form of interest would not wish to work to earn more with Uncle Sam taking still another three cents out of every additional dollar. But with interest income 3 percent or less of GDP (a bit higher percentage of national income) we would seem a long way from serious worry about that.

AND INFLATION?

We are also told that large deficits will cause inflation. The first answer to this is that we have had some large deficits in the last decade and inflation has declined sharply. It is running currently at no more than 3 percent by official measure, and is probably less, perhaps zero with full adjustment for product improvement. Some inflation measures were in fact close to zero by official count, at least momentarily, in the summer of 1993. The time series relation between deficits and inflation in the United States has indeed generally been negative; bigger deficits have come with less inflation and smaller deficits with more inflation. To be fair, however, this reflects primarily the effect of the economy on the deficit, rather than the deficit on the economy. In recessions, inflation tends to be less and, with lesser tax revenues and greater outlays for unemployment benefits, deficits are larger. In booms, inflation may be more, but tax revenues are greater and unemployment benefits less, so that deficits are less.

An appropriate test of the effect of deficits on inflation, or on any other economic variables, would have to abstract from the reverse effect of those variables on the deficit. One way to get at this is to work with a measure of the deficit that is not affected by the fluctuations of the economy. For this purpose we may use what has variously been called the structural, the cyclically adjusted, or the "high-employment" budget. This indicates what tax revenues, outlays, and the deficit *would* be if the economy were on some fixed path as, say, at 6 percent unemployment. The size of the high-employment deficit may then be a measure of fiscal stimulus. But larger high-employment deficits have not been associated with more inflation.

The reason for this negative finding brings us closer to the fundamental relation of government deficits and government debt to the economy. That depends very considerably on the state of the economy, whether it is zooming along at top speed or is in a sluggish, slack-resources, unemployment mode. Recognizing this will lead us to the conclusion—however shocking to some—that deficits can be good for us. They will be good if they generate purchasing power for the products of American business that would otherwise be lacking. In general, deficits can be too small as well as too large. And for most of the past half-century, including right now, contrary to the conventional wisdom, we will find that deficits have been too small. Far from struggling to reduce the deficit, as President Clinton has constrained himself to do, or making demagogic appeals for zero deficits (or even surpluses to "pay off" the debt), as has Mr. Perot, we should be looking for the most productive ways to increase it.

ARE DEFICITS IRRELEVANT?

There is a school of thought, led by Harvard's Robert Barro, which argues that deficits essentially do not matter. This is not my argument. What Barro and his numerous but minority followers among economists claim is that financing government expenditures by borrowing and by (at least non-distortionary "lump-sum") taxes are equivalent in their effects on the economy. This proposition was labelled "Ricardian equivalence" after the great classical economist, David Ricardo, who first suggested the possibility, although he himself rejected it. If government expenditures are financed by borrowing instead of by taxes, tax payers will have greater current after-tax incomes. Ricardian equivalence asserts they will not spend their extra income. They will rather set it aside—save it—to pay the future taxes necessary to service the resulting debt, or leave it to their children to pay those taxes. Government debt financing will thus induce no more spending than tax financing. And it will induce no less saving, since the increased public dis-saving of the higher deficit will be offset by the increased private saving induced by the knowledge that there will be more taxes to pay in the future.

The arguments against Ricardian equivalence are myriad: the difference between the borrowing and lending costs of government and those of private agents (who frequently have liquidity constraints); the lack of certainty or even knowledge by any of us that future taxes will in fact be higher in the foreseeable future; the possibility that somebody else, including the parents of our children's spouses—the other grandparents of our grandchildren—may be providing for the future taxes; the chance that we may not have any children or may consider them worthless and not worth providing for if we do. But I leave that debate to the economics journals, which have filled many pages with it.

HOW DEFICITS DO MATTER

We return then to the mainstream argument that deficits do matter, and we will ascertain how. Most simply, deficits, as opposed to government outlays financed by taxes, do matter because they add to the purchasing power and aggregate demand of the private sector. People or businesses are likely to spend more when they have a higher income after taxes—or when they hold government securities—than they are when all they have is a receipt for payment of taxes. All of our economic theory and empirical evidence indicate that people with more income and wealth, other things equal, will spend more.

That increases in the real value of the government debt to the private sector increase consumption and aggregate demand is old neoclassical economics, a line of reasoning to be found in works of Gottfried Haberler, now at the conservative American Enterprise Institute after a long and distinguished career, and A.C. Pigou, the prominent "classical" target of Keynes at Cambridge. The Keynesian argument is parallel, that real deficits increase consumption by adding to current real disposable income; Keynes also included changes in the value of wealth as an argument of his consumption function, warning that ignoring them in times when they were changing would be perilous.

Failure to take into account the huge increase in debt held by the public during World War II—recall that the debt/GNP ratio was well over 100 percent in 1946—was a major factor in the alarmist, erroneous predictions that the end of the war would bring on a major recession. And that failure was part of the background and motivation for the path-breaking work of Nobel laureates Milton Friedman and Franco Modigliani in developing our modern theory of the consumption function. Wealth, or the permanent income to be expected from that wealth, is a critical determinant of consumption expenditures.

If we doubt that theory, we can try a little introspection. Suppose I could arrange with Lloyd Bentsen, our Secretary of the Treasury, for each reader of this book to be given

$100,000 of new Treasury bills. How many would feel poorer? How many would ignore their new holdings and spend nothing more? And how many might just buy a new car or take a more expensive vacation trip? If even some fell into that last category, the result would be higher consumption expenditures, and more business to those producing the additional goods or services purchased. But this new accumulation or additional holding of Treasury bills—or other Treasury securities, or cash to the extent that the Federal Reserve buys some of the additional debt—is exactly what occurs when the government runs a deficit.

There is one important qualification, too often overlooked. Would those holding $100,000 in Treasury bills today feel richer and hence spend more now than they would have a year ago if they had then been holding $99,000? There is a one-word caution, "Inflation." If prices today are 3 percent higher than a year ago, then today's $100,000 is the equivalent, roughly, of $97,000 in last year's purchasing power. Those debt holders are now not richer by $1,000 but, in real terms, poorer by $2,000.

We may be expected to feel richer and spend more only to the extent that the deficit raised our wealth in government securities by more than enough to keep up with inflation. A deficit is a *real* deficit only to the extent that it adds to the real value, that is, the value in constant dollars, of our holdings of government debt. We may view the loss in real value of outstanding debt due to inflation as an "inflation tax" levied by the government on debt holders, thus reducing that real deficit. Another way of looking at this is to see that of the $180 billion of interest payments swelling the nominal deficit, some $90 billion represents the amount the government finds it necessary to pay, because of higher nominal interest rates, to compensate bond holders for their inflation losses.

THE SHORT RUN: IMPACT ON CONSUMPTION, OUTPUT, AND EMPLOYMENT

While the greater wealth the public holds in government debt as a result of deficits will induce more consumption, greater deficits are actually expected to be accompanied by less consumption. This is a consequence of the fact that recessions and associated unemployment reduce consumption and also, as we have noted, increase deficits. We have, therefore, to avoid confusing cause and effect—the effect of deficits on the economy and the effect of the economy on the deficit.

To ascertain the effect of an independent increase in the deficit—not one brought on by the decline of the economy— we again need a "cyclically adjusted" or structural or "high-employment," that is, fixed-unemployment budget. This would indicate what, given tax rates and expenditures, the deficit *would be*, aside from fluctuations of the economy, if, for example, unemployment were fixed at 6 percent. Further, it is only real increases in wealth in the form of government debt held by the public that can be expected to affect consumption. We should hence also adjust the deficit for the loss in the real value of the debt due to changes in the price level.

The impact of deficits on the economy should then be found in the relation between an inflation-adjusted and cyclically adjusted deficit and the economic variables with which we are concerned. I have accordingly constructed[6] time series of what I call the price-adjusted, high-employment deficit. And I have worked these into simple charts and tables and more rigorous least-squares regressions as well as, more recently, VARs (vector autoregressions). These last put together past and current values of the underlying variables and try to estimate their relations and interrelations without preconditions or confining specifications as to lags or what determines what. The results have confirmed, as I have tested the relations for robustness over time as well as to variations in formulations, that deficits, over the past three decades at least, have been good for us.

Specifically, we have found that higher values of the price-adjusted, high-employment deficit, taken as a percentage of GNP or GDP, have been associated with more rapid subse-

---

[6] Again with Paul J. Pieper of the University of Illinois at Chicago, my collaborator in many of these investigations.

quent growth in real product, as seen in Figure 5.2.[7] And since more rapid growth in real product is associated with decreases in unemployment, or at least lesser increases, it comes as no surprise that we have also found that larger deficits, or smaller surpluses, have been associated with less subsequent unemployment, as shown in Figure 5.3.

There is one condition that must have been necessary for this result. There must have been slack resources over most of the last 30 years showing these relations. Unemployment could not have been reduced by bigger deficits if it were already at its rock-bottom, full-employment level. And output could not have increased faster if there were no additional workers and no additional capacity for increased production. Sadly, this slack-resource condition was met. It must be recognized that, except for wartime—unemployment reached the 3 percent level during the Vietnam War—we have rarely, if ever, had truly full employment.

Herein is a vital caution to President Clinton and the Congress as they put into place a program for economic recovery and sustained, high-investment growth. We entered 1993 with unemployment still over 7 percent. By August 1993 it had dropped slightly to 6.7 percent, but employment was still lagging. Most forecasts, including those used by the Office of Management and Budget, the Congressional Budget Office, and the Clinton administration itself, indicated that this unemployment rate would, at best, continue to move down only very slowly. Yet, the economic program Clinton presented in his February 17, 1993 address to Congress proposed reducing the structural deficit by $55 billion from 1993 to 1994.[8] Was this a time for the restraint of deficit reduction, or for the stimulus of *more* government spending—preferably for public investment—and *lower* taxes?

---

[7]More sophisticated statistical presentation of this relation may be found in my 1986 book, *How Real Is the Federal Deficit?* (New York: The Free Press), and a number of articles in the *American Economic Review,* the *Journal of Economic Perspectives,* and other journals and volumes.

[8]The economic plan being pushed through Congress in the summer of 1993 called for a cumulative total of $500 billion of deficit reduction over a five-year period.

Figure 5.2   *Changes in Price-Adjusted, High-Employment Deficit and Subsequent Real GDP, 1961–1991*

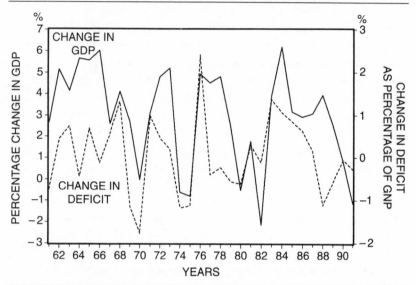

Sources: Price-adjusted, high-employment deficit is derived from estimates of 6 percent unemployment surplus furnished by Michael Webb of the Government Division of the Bureau of Economic Analysis. Price adjustment by author and Paul J. Pieper reduces deficit by product of inflation rate (as indicated by GNP implicit price deflator) and net debt held by the public. Gross national product, gross domestic product, in current and 1987 dollars, unemployment, gross private domestic investment, federal and total tangible government investment, government expenditures on education from U.S. Department of Commerce, *National Income and Product Accounts of the United States*, vol. 2, 1959–1988 (Washington: U.S. Government Printing Office); 1992 and subsequent years from NIPA tapes, *Economic Report of the President, 1993*, or issues of the *Survey of Current Business*. Change in total fixed reproducible capital, used in measure of real total national saving, from "Summary Fixed Reproducible Tangible Wealth Series, 1925–90," *Survey of Current Business,* January 1992, updated to 1991 with unpublished data furnished by John Musgrave of the Bureau of Economic Analysis.

This fundamental fact of excess unemployment may be challenged by devotees of the pernicious "natural rate" of unemployment or "nonaccelerating-inflation-rate of unemployment (NAIRU)."[9] They may find 6 percent or 6.5 percent or even the 7+ percent of the last year of the Bush administration to be natural. They may think that in our perfect market economy whatever is must be optimal and natural. I recall

---

[9]I will challenge these devotees in Chapter 8.

Figure 5.3 *Price-Adjusted, High-Employment Deficit and
Subsequent Change in Unemployment, 1961–1991*

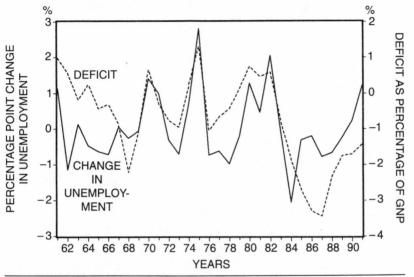

Sources: See Figure 5.2.

the anecdote about the graduate student who in January 1983
wrote on the board the depth-of-recession news flash from the
Bureau of Labor Statistics. "The *natural* rate of unemployment has just reached 10.7 percent."

But I will maintain that involuntary unemployment due to
a lack of aggregate demand or purchasing power is a fundamental fact of our economy, as confirmed by these effects of
deficits. And this fundamental fact makes all the difference,
refuting most arguments for reducing the deficit at this time,
and exposes the error of the conventional wisdom of too many,
although not all, macroeconomic theorists.

THE LONG RUN: IMPACT ON NATIONAL SAVING

The fact that increases in the real, structural deficit
have usually triggered or increased growth in output and led
to reductions in unemployment becomes central to the one
possible legitimate argument that deficits may be too large.

This does not relate to their current effect. As long as there is some slack in the economy, fiscal stimulus in the form of bigger deficits will raise output and employment in the short term. But, it is insisted, they reduce "national saving." In so doing, they reduce the capital we will have in the future and hence reduce future product. That is—or would be, if it were true—the real burden that deficits place on our children and grandchildren and indeed, except for those near the end of their lives, on all of us.

Is it true though? Do our deficits reduce national saving and investment, or capital accumulation? There is one simplistic argument that gives the false impression that this is inevitable. Conventional gross national saving, GS, is defined as the sum of private saving—personal saving, PS, and business saving, BS (undistributed corporate profits plus capital consumption allowances)—and public saving or the consolidated federal, state, and local budget surpluses, FS plus SLS, as was illustrated in Table 3.1. The total of gross national saving (except for a statistical discrepancy) is identically equal to the total of gross investment, GI.

$$GS \equiv PS + BS + FS + SLS\,(+SD) \equiv GI$$

or, in actual billions of dollars for 1992,

$$741 \equiv 239 + 748 - 276 + 7\,(+23) \equiv 741$$

Deficits are then seen as negative surpluses, or negative public saving that offsets private positive saving. Bigger federal deficits constitute a still greater negative value to FS and hence mean less total or national saving, GS, and less gross investment, GI, or less accumulation of capital for the future. Reducing "the deficit," reducing the absolute value of that -276 to, say, -176, would raise national saving and investment. All this may seem apparent from the identity above and in Table 3.3, where I have, however, modified the conventional national income and product account to include public investment, both tangible and intangible, in public saving.

The simplistic argument is, alas, just too simple. It entails the elementary fallacy of assuming *ceteris paribus,* other things the same. Imagine more realistically, for example, that the federal deficit is reduced—FS is made less negative—by cutting grants to state and local governments, which have been running about $180 billion per year. Would this not immediately reduce state and local government surpluses, SLS, and thus offset the reduction in the federal deficit or algebraically higher value of FS?

Or suppose the federal deficit is reduced by raising income taxes. This would reduce disposable personal income and surely reduce personal saving, PS, the difference between disposable personal income and consumption, even if, as is likely, consumption were also reduced. So here we would have another offset to the increase in public saving, or reduction in public dis-saving. Similarly, an increase in corporate profits taxes would reduce undistributed corporate profits and thus reduce business saving, BS. And a like consequence, it should be noted, would flow from a reduction in government expenditures, either in transfer payments like social security benefits or in government outlays for goods and services. In both events, disposable income and private saving would be reduced. A decline in BS and PS would at least partly offset the algebraic increase in FS.

It is clear that the increase in national saving constituted by the decreased dis-saving of a lesser federal budget deficit will be offset and *may* be fully offset or more than fully offset by other *reductions* in saving. How can we ascertain whether this will be so? The answer may be found in looking at aggregate saving's identical twin, aggregate investment.

LOOKING AT INVESTMENT

A nation invests either by accumulating its own real assets on its own soil or by acquiring claims to assets in the rest of the world. As was noted earlier, gross investment is the sum of gross private domestic investment and net foreign investment.

$$GI \equiv GPDI + NFI$$

As shown again in Table 3.1 for 1992 in billions of dollars

$$741 = 796 - 55$$

And gross national saving, GS, we have noted, is identically equal to—can be neither more nor less than—gross investment. Whether national saving would be raised or lowered by a reduction in federal deficits can then better be considered by finding its effects on the components of the other side of the identity, gross investment.

By far the largest element here is gross private domestic investment, the sum of business and nonprofit institution expenditures on new equipment and structures, construction of new housing, and increases in business inventories. Would the cuts in consumption and government expenditures for goods and services result in more or less private domestic investment? If we cut our purchases of new cars, is that going to lead the automobile industry to spend more on new facilities—or less? If our disposable income is cut, will we buy more or fewer new houses?

I may seem to be loading the questions; the answer is not that obvious. Classical economists and the conventional wisdom would argue that, if the government is borrowing less, interest rates will be lower and this will stimulate more business investment and purchase of new houses. But, as I asked in Chapter 3, will this positive effect outweigh the negative effect of lower incomes and lower sales to ultimate consumers?

A half-century ago this issue was examined by Oscar Lange in a seminal review of Keynes's *General Theory*.[10] He pointed out that there was an "optimal propensity to consume" that would maximize investment. This would be reached when the stimulative effect of more consumption on investment was eventually just balanced by the increasing negative effects of higher interest rates.

---

[10]"The Rate of Interest and the Optimal Propensity to Consume," *Economica*, February 1938, new series 5, pp. 12–32. Reprinted in American Economic Association, *Readings in Business Cycle Theory* (Philadelphia: Blakiston, 1944), pp. 169–192.

What happens is that, as consumption begins its increase from low levels, the developing pressure on capacity stimulates investment. There is initially little rise in recession-interest rates and hence little negative effect on investment. As full employment is approached, more consumption begins to crowd out investment simply because there is no more capacity to increase both consumption and investment.

Once the economy is at—or close to—full employment, since output and income can no longer be rising rapidly, if at all, the only way for there to be significantly more saving is for there to be an inducement to people to save larger proportions of their income. That inducement can come from higher interest rates. These therefore may rise as business struggles to get the funds—which can only be obtained by inducing this higher saving proportion—to finance additional capital to increase capacity. But these higher interest rates increasingly choke off investment.

Thus, whether more consumption or more government expenditures for goods and services "crowd out" domestic private investment may depend upon how close the economy is to full employment. If we are at full employment–or some people's "natural rate"—so that output cannot be increased, then it is clear that, aside from getting goods from the rest of the world, more output going to consumption or government must mean less output going to private investment. If we are not at full employment, the outcome of changes in budget deficits, changing consumption, and/or government spending is not clear. We can, however, look at the historical facts.

Here again I call upon my charts, tables, and regressions. These do show clear results, illustrated in Figure 5.4. Larger inflation-adjusted, structural deficits have been associated with *more* subsequent gross private domestic investment; smaller deficits have been associated with less investment. My multiple regression results add the information that easier money or monetary stimulus, as measured by increases in the real monetary base, has also been associated with increases in real output *and* domestic investment. The remedy to any increases in interest rates would thus appear to be

Figure 5.4   *Price-Adjusted, High-Employment Deficit and Subsequent Gross Private Domestic Investment, 1959–1991*

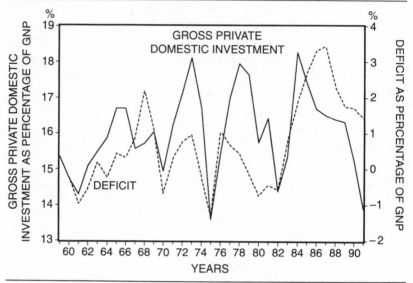

Sources: See Figure 5.2.

supportive, stimulatory monetary policy by the Federal Reserve.

This, though, still does not tell the whole story. Recall that gross investment includes net foreign investment. And net foreign investment is very largely net exports or, a bit more generally, the current account surplus in our balance of international payments. If we export more than we import, to the extent we do not give foreigners' payments to us back to them, we acquire foreign assets. We thus have net foreign investment. But if we import more than we export, we pay for this excess by giving foreigners net additional claims, in debt or equity, on us. We have negative net foreign investment, reducing total gross investment.

Will not increased deficits stimulate the demand for all goods, foreign as well as domestic, and thus increase imports and reduce net foreign investment? Indeed they will. And reductions in the deficit would reduce imports—perhaps by causing a recession—and raise net foreign investment!

Whether reducing deficits raises or reduces national saving then depends upon the balance of the two effects, the increase in net foreign investment and the reduction in gross private domestic investment.

Once more, we can turn to the data. The results of statistical analysis, while not as sharp as in the case of domestic investment alone, challenge the argument that reducing deficits is likely to raise national saving. The historical record has been the opposite. Larger, real structural deficits have been associated with more national saving and smaller deficits with less.

DEFICITS, TOTAL NATIONAL SAVING, AND OUR FUTURE

The statistical relation involving the conventional, narrow measure of national saving, it must be acknowledged, is not very strong. It is strengthened in a major way, however, when we recognize that what is relevant for our future, and that of our children and grandchildren, is not merely the accumulation of capital in the form of gross private domestic investment and net investment in the rest of the world. Of vital significance is public investment in all of the tangible infrastructure on which private industry depends, as well as household investment in durable goods and all investment, public and private, in the human and intangible investment of education and training and research and the basic services of public security on which social living depends.

Increased federal deficits may well go toward financing increased public investment. They have apparently done so in the past, if insufficiently. This is shown in Figure 5.5, relating the inflation-adjusted, structural deficit to federal tangible investment, in Figure 5.6, relating it to total government tangible investment, in Figure 5.7, relating it to total government expenditures on education, and in Figure 5.8, relating it to total real government investment, all as percentages of GNP.

As a start to measuring this broader effect of deficits, I have

Figure 5.5 *Changes in Price-Adjusted, High-Employment Deficit and Real Federal Tangible Investment, 1960–1991*

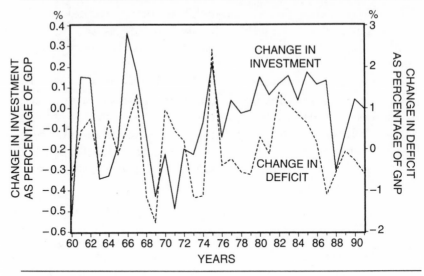

Sources: See Figure 5.2.

Figure 5.6 *Changes in Price-Adjusted, High-Employment Deficit and Real Total Government Tangible Investment, 1960–1991*

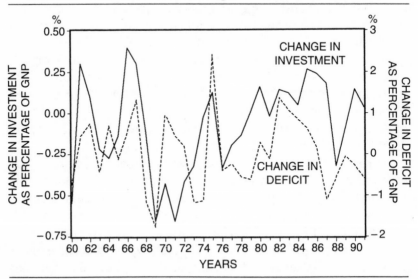

Sources: See Figure 5.2.

Figure 5.7 *Changes in Price-Adjusted, High-Employment Deficit and Real Total Government Expenditures on Education, 1960–1991*

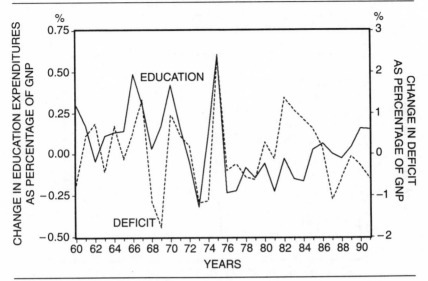

Sources: See Figure 5.2.

Figure 5.8 *Changes in Price-Adjusted, High-Employment Deficit and Real Total Government Investment, 1961–1991*

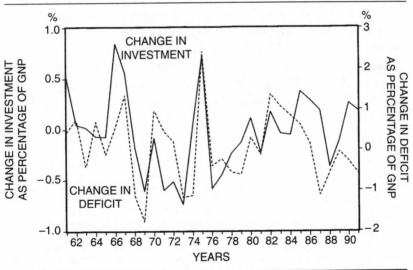

Sources: See Figure 5.2.

117

Figure 5.9   *Changes in Price-Adjusted, High-Employment Deficit and Subsequent Real Total National Saving, 1961–1991*

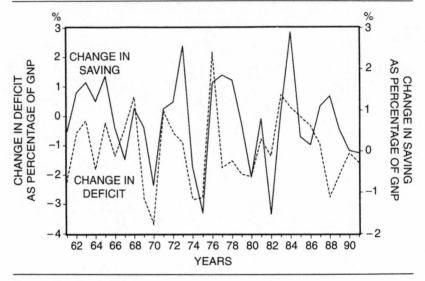

Sources: See Figure 5.2.

related our real, structural deficits to expanded measures of national saving. In series for national saving inclusive of government and household tangible investment, I find again a sharp positive relation with our deficits, as may be readily seen in Figure 5.9. Larger price-adjusted, high-employment deficits have been associated with more, not less national saving.[11]

---

[11]I have set forth these findings on the relation between deficits and saving in more rigorous fashion in: "Deficits: Which, How Much and So What?," *The American Economic Review,* vol. 72, May 1992, pp. 295–298; "National Saving and Budget Deficits," *Review of Economics and Statistics,* November 1993; "U.S. National Saving and Budget Deficits," in Gerald Epstein and Herbert Gintis, eds., *The Political Economy of Investment, Saving and Finance: A Global Perspective,* A Project of the World Institute for Development and Economic Research (WIDER), The United Nations University, Helsinki, Finland, 1993, to be published by the Cambridge University Press; and "Real Government Saving and the Future," *Journal of Economic Behavior and Organization,* vol. 23, January 1994.

Given the state of our economy, present deficits are not too large. They can, should, and probably will be brought down as we reduce unemployment, speed economic growth, and achieve a prosperous economy.

Real, structural deficits have helped and not hurt output, employment, consumption, and well-being in the present. They have also entailed more, not less investment in our future.

President Clinton, in advancing a broad-based program for investment and economic growth, has stated explicitly, "Deficit reduction is not an end in itself." The purpose of deficit reduction is rather to help provide for our future by increasing national saving and investment. But he and all of us must then beware of the danger that deficit-cutting measures will curtail or reduce conventionally measured gross private domestic or business investment, household investment, and the public investment in physical capital and in people that he sees, correctly, as vital to that future.

CHAPTER 6

Helping Baby and Grandma: Myths about Social Security and Other Intergenerational Transfers

> ". . . [E]very newborn baby starts out with a debt of over $50,000 because he or she will owe that much more in taxes than he or she will ever receive in government benefits."—Warren B. Rudman's and Paul Tsongas's *The Concord Coalition,* initial statement, September 1992, p. 12.

> To the "young people of this country: give them their future back!"—Message of Rudman and Tsongas on MacNeil-Lehrer News Hour, PBS, June 22, 1993.

> ". . . [I]f there is no change in the net taxes paid by current generations, future generations will have to pay net taxes equal to 71% of their lifetime incomes."—Lawrence J. Kotlikoff, author of "Generational Accounting: Knowing Who Pays, and When, for What We Spend," in *Harvard Business Review,* May–June 1993, p. 105.

And more statements that have charged the political debate:

- The share of the federal debt of each baby born today is almost $17,000.
- The elderly are threatened because the Treasury keeps borrowing from the social security retirement trust fund in order to finance the deficit in all its other operations.

- "Entitlements" are too high. They are the largest and most rapidly growing portion of the federal budget. We have gotten overly generous to the elderly on social security and should tax their benefits more or cut their cost-of-living allowances.

What truth and relevance do these statements contain? Very little, but we need a frame of reference and analytical tools to evaluate them.

THE DEBT OF AMERICAN BABIES

Let us start with one of the simple propositions, about the share of the federal debt acquired by each newborn baby. That is arrived at by dividing the *gross* public debt, approaching $4.4 trillion at the end of the 1993 fiscal year, by the population of the United States, approximately 260 million. To begin with, the numerator is misleading. The gross debt, as explained in Chapter 4 (see note 14), includes over a trillion dollars of federal "debt" held by the various government trust funds, including those for social security, and elsewhere within the government itself. The debt "held by the public" is only some $3.3 trillion. Although politicians like to quote the larger figure, it is simply not applicable to the shares for newborn babies. In fact, even of that $3.3 trillion, some $300 billion is held by the public only in the technical sense that it is held by the Federal Reserve banks, which are legally public corporations. Of course, they are actually a branch of government and their income from the interest on Treasury security holdings essentially goes right back into the Treasury.

The issue, though, is more fundamental than that of the particular numbers. The basic point follows from one I made earlier. The debt of the federal government is largely an asset of the American people, who own the great bulk of the Treasury bills, notes, and bonds that constitute the debt. It could just as well be said, therefore, that each newborn baby acquires—directly or through his or her parents—assets equal to his or her share of that debt. Perhaps the much decried deficit, which adds each year to the debt, is just ensuring that new babies are at least as well endowed as those that have come before!

HOW ONE GENERATION TAKES CARE OF ANOTHER

Intergenerational justice is a vital issue in any society. Without care, infants and the very young cannot even survive. And without some kind of external care, the elderly would be hard pressed to survive, certainly to survive in a fashion most of us feel they merit. Parents ordinarily provide primary care for the very young. In the cases of many single- or zero-parent families and others in poverty, this care is not available, and society takes up some of the slack. Societal help is vital, at least for those in poverty, in the area of health care, including prenatal and infant care. Society also intervenes in a major way by offering the elementary and secondary education without which, it has become increasingly clear, the rising generation cannot function economically in the modern world. In the United States, at least, it appears that a college education has become almost essential for economic success, and no more than one-third of our population is completing that.[1]

At the other end of the generational ladder, the elderly are living longer, as modern medicine helps raise life expectancies. What with the aged and the young and those unemployed or out of the labor force while providing child care, less than half of the population is engaged in market work to support more than half who are not. Specifically, 120 million people are working and 140 million are not.

---

[1]Robert Reich, President Clinton's Secretary of Labor, writes, "Today, the weekly earnings of full-time workers over 25 who are college graduates are more than 50 percent above the earnings of otherwise similar workers who are simply high-school graduates."—*New York Times,* July 20, 1993, Op-Ed page.

To a considerable extent—to a greater extent in recent decades, with the development of private pension programs, than in earlier times—the elderly feel that they are providing for themselves. From the standpoint of the elderly as a group or the economy as a whole, there is a certain self-deception here. Aside from some real property that they may have, particularly houses, the elderly provide themselves only with pieces of paper—stocks, bonds, pension and insurance checks, bank deposits, and cash under the mattress. Society must produce the goods and services that these pieces of paper can be used to buy. Otherwise they amount to just that—pieces of paper.

Before social security was established in 1935, and before there was much in the way of private pension funds, many of the elderly worked until they died; others who survived to an age or state of health where they could no longer earn their own living were cared for, if not always adequately, by their children. In one sense, social security merely inserted a government intermediary in the care of aged parents by children. Instead of working children supporting parents directly, they now contribute to a social security fund which in turn pays out, not to them, but to those parents. The parents may think that they are being supported by their own past financial contributions. That is a matter of financial legerdemain. In any meaningful economic sense, the past contributions of the current aged parents were used to support *their* parents. By contributing then, they refrained from buying the equivalent of some of what they had produced. Their parents were able to use their social security checks to buy that equivalent themselves. The children then had worked to support their parents but had used the intermediary of the social security system to finance that support.

INTERGENERATIONAL TRANSFERS—AT A POINT IN TIME AND ACROSS POINTS IN TIME

There are two issues on intergenerational transfers, sometimes surprisingly confused by good economic theorists.

One is the transfer from one generation living now to another generation living now, as when young adults support either their children or their parents, with or without the intermediation or coercion of government. The other is the transfer somehow of wealth from people living at one period of time to people living at another. The second is less easily accomplished than the first. Failures of the market mechanism in implementing preferences on such transfers play a major role in bringing on recessions and unemployment.

Assume, for example, that a person decides not to buy a new house in Illinois now but rather to save the money to buy into a retirement home in Florida 20 years from now. The market may not provide the mechanism, through sufficiently fluctuating interest rates, building trade wages, or what have you, to avoid loss of jobs in Illinois now, and whatever loss occurs will not be balanced by increased jobs now in Florida or anywhere else. The same problem arises if we "save" to bequeath to our children or grandchildren.

We can take bread out of one mouth today and give it to another today. We cannot save bread to give it to ourselves or our children or grandchildren, 50 years from now. The best we can do to make such a transfer is to build an oven that we hope will still be functioning 50 years from now, or train a new baker now who will still be plying his trade then. As I have indicated earlier and shall repeat, the only way we can provide now for the future is to create the human and/or physical capital, public or private, that will be used in the future.

THOSE NET TAXES AND BURDENS ON FUTURE GENERATIONS

Armed with these perceptions, we can evaluate some of the statements at the beginning of this chapter. First, what about that $50,000 in taxes in excess of benefits about which Rudman and Tsongas would have us worry? It is hard to know what to make of this until we know what the Concord twins mean by "benefits." Do they include education, public roads, police protection, a judicial system, national defense? If they do not, but include only cash or transfer payments like unemployment benefits, welfare payments, and social security, they make a meaningless comparison between taxes and "benefits." Remember, as was shown in Table 3.2, that government gross capital expenditures came to $530 billion in 1992; government education investment alone amounted to $262 billion. The gross total translates to over $2,000 per man, woman, and child. The present value of these expenditures, if continued indefinitely into the future, would easily match the Rudman–Tsongas $50,000 "benefits" shortfall.

Further, what does Kotlikoff mean by saying that "future generations" will have to pay net taxes equal to 71 percent of their lifetime incomes? His scenario is one in which those now alive pay taxes and receive benefits at currently set schedules and those not yet born will eventually "pay off" the resulting debt, along with the interest that has accumulated on that debt in the interim. There are several wrong or critically misleading assumptions that Kotlikoff uses in arriving at his scary 71 percent.

First, as he points out, his projections apply if tax rates and benefit schedules for all those now alive do not change over their lifetimes. But if Kotlikoff's unbalanced scenarios did materialize, as people lived too long or retired too early or received too much medical care or too expensive an education, it is reasonable to expect that somewhere well before the last person now alive passes on, tax rates, social security benefits, retirement ages, or the like would be corrected. That is neither reason nor justification for making those corrections now. It may be—consider the stale bread problem—unfeasible or impossible to make them now.

Second, Kotlikoff fails to include in his intergenerational accounting the full value of all the governmental services received by each generation or the extent to which taxes are used, directly or indirectly, to invest in that capital, human or physical, public or private, which is the one real way to take care of the future.

Third, the notion that the debt incurred by current genera-

tions has somehow to be paid off *eventually* by future generations is a confusing, or confused, effort to use a mathematical
principle of solvency[2] where it does not apply. The fact is
that in an economy with a growing population and, a fortiori,
growing income per capita as well (both of which conditions
can certainly be expected to apply to the United States), there
is no reason why the federal debt cannot continue to be rolled
over and to grow, at least with the nation's growing income.
If this happened the debt—and interest payments, if interest
rates did not change—per dollar of income would remain the
same. The federal debt of 52 cents per dollar of gross national
product—$3,247 billion ÷ $6,295 billion at the end of the
1993 fiscal year—would still be 52 cents per dollar of gross
national product. The sky, which has not fallen under current
conditions, would remain where it is.

What Kotlikoff and others should address is not the "net
taxes" to be paid on a particular, arbitrary set of assumptions,
but what private choice and the government are doing to affect the distribution of income and welfare at any one point
in time and what they are doing to affect that distribution
over time. The latter, except to the limited extent that bread
lasts more than a day, cannot be accomplished except by affecting the accumulation of capital, human and physical.

THE ARBITRARINESS OF OUR MEASURES AGAIN— ALL THOSE CONTINGENT LIABILITIES

Kotlikoff has made a point well worth making as to
the arbitrariness of contemporary measures of the debt and
deficits. This arbitrariness spills over into the evaluations of
the effect of conventional measures on intergenerational
transfers or distribution of welfare. He points out, for example, that contributions to social insurance—payroll taxes—
might be called premiums, or loans to the government, com-

---

[2]Technically, the condition of "transversality."

pulsory though they may be. The social security checks of retirees might then be classified as repayment, with interest, of these loans. This classification change would make literally trillions of dollars of implicit obligations of the federal government, in the form of retirement benefit commitments, explicit debt.

If the present value of the unfunded liability, or net social security debt for those currently in the social security system[3] (the "closed group" cited in note 5), were included, we would increase the official, explicit gross debt of $4.4 trillion by $7.6 trillion.[4] But if we take into account the taxes to be paid in, as well as the benefits to be paid out, relating to all those in the social security system over the next 75 years (the "open group" of note 5), the net social security debt is reduced to $1.9 trillion. It would take an increase in payroll taxes of only 1.46 percentage points, or reduction in benefits amounting to that much, to eliminate this debt.[5]

---

[3] Approximately the difference, for current participants, between (1) the present value of total benefits that will be paid in the future and (2) the sum of current assets of the social security funds and the present value of future contributions to them.

[4] For those who want to be frightened with misleading figures, if just the present value of all of the prospective benefits to those currently in the social security system were included, without taking into account expected future taxes, we would increase the official, explicit gross debt of $4.4 trillion by $16.5 trillion! It is hard to see the economic relevance of a total of payouts that does not net out associated receipts or, from the standpoint of the public, benefits that do not net out the payments necessary to receive them.

[5] Harry C. Ballantyne, chief actuary of the Social Security Administration, commenting on this paragraph, explains,

[A]s of October 1, 1993, our current estimate of the present value of future expenditures for the Old-Age and Survivors Insurance and Disability Insurance (OASDI) program over the next 75 years is $16.5 trillion on a 'closed' group basis and $20.6 trillion on an 'open' group basis. The 'closed' group consists of all persons now aged 15 and over, who are, or may become, workers and/or beneficiaries over the next 75 years. The open group, therefore, includes persons not yet born, as well as persons under age 15. The present value of assets, including future tax contributions, is $8.9 trillion on a closed group basis, and $18.7 trillion on an open group basis. The unfunded liability, or deficit, for the Social Security program is, therefore, $7.6 trillion on a closed group basis and $1.9 trillion on an open group basis.

Unlike private pension plans, coverage is universal and compulsory under the Social Security program. Therefore, it is not necessary and not intended

I have argued that these and other "contingency" obligations of the Treasury, largely insurance and insurance guarantees, should be taken into account. They should not, however, be given the same status in the measures as formal obligations and debt. Their very contingency lessens their impact on the economic behavior with which we are concerned.

Recall that by conventional measure the deficit is the increase in the debt. In 1983, by raising premium schedules and raising the age for receiving benefits, the changes in the social security law lowered the net "debt" to those then in the Old-Age and Survivors and Disability Insurance program by about $700 billion in one fell swoop.[6] Should we consider this reduction in debt an equivalent budget surplus? An excess of $700 billion of conventional, current taxes over outlays in 1983, or any year since, would have wrecked the economy, entailing an enormous reduction in after-tax income and consequently large reduction in private purchasing power.

In fact, this actuarial change in social security net wealth had no perceptible effect on economic behavior. Most of those in the social security system were hardly aware of it. Those who were aware probably did not believe that, when their time to receive benefits arrived, the current changes in the law would have made much difference. Instead, people may rather have sensed that what they receive in retirement will depend on how prosperous the country is then, and what share of that prosperity they can use the political process to obtain for themselves.

---

that the Social Security program be fully funded on a closed group basis. The long-range actuarial status of the Social Security program is measured on an open group basis, which takes account of all future contributions, and future benefits, over the next 75 years for persons who will enter employment in the next 75 years (including persons not yet born), as well as for current workers and beneficiaries. On this basis, the long-range unfunded obligations over the next 75 years are estimated to be 1.46 percent of the present value of the future taxable payroll over the next 75 years.

[6]Estimates from Stephen Goss of the Office of the Actuary of the Social Security Administration.

HOW TO GIVE THEIR FUTURE BACK TO THE YOUNG

As for the young, to whom Rudman and Tsongas would give back their future, that future will depend little on the share of the debt they are presumed to have to liquidate by paying taxes in excess of benefits. As I have proposed, the connection may prove quite the opposite of that suggested by the Concord Coalition and others. Greater public debt adds to private purchasing power and may finance the creation of more public capital. It may go with greater GDP, more saving and investment, and more for our young, not less.

One place to start giving the young back their future is with prenatal care, which should be part of the American health program for all fetuses conceived. Next are adequate parent training and health care and child care and education for all our youths. This would include everything from adequate diet and childhood disease immunizations to providing neighborhoods to grow up in that are drug free and crime free.

We should be offering top-quality education to all of our young, bringing out the best of which all of them are capable. Generations of school dropouts and functional illiterates must no longer characterize major portions of our school-age children. Their lack of productivity imposes heavy costs on our economy and society. And our better students, in good suburban schools, should no longer score last, as they have scored in comparison with students in Western Europe and Asia on similar tests in math and science given to 13-year-olds (as well as those of other ages).

To give the young a future we should have apprentice and training programs and other measures to offer a smooth transition from successful school performance to success on the job. There should be college education for all those, regardless of current financial situation, who have the will and capacity to benefit from it. We should have a finance and credit system that facilitates borrowing and debt to pay for such education as well as the investment by young adults in their own homes. This investment, and the jobs they hold, will give them an early stake in a productive society. And we should have continued investment in the protection and improvement of our vital environment of air, land, and water and in the research and new ideas as well as new hardware and technology, publicly or privately financed, that will make each generation clearly more productive and richer than the one that came before it.

Such a positive program to give the future back to the young is little fostered by misguided efforts to reduce their share of the debt or future taxes. It is very likely impaired, given the political process as well as economic dynamics, by know-nothing efforts to cut or even eliminate government budget deficits. These efforts make it very difficult, if not impossible, to undertake precisely the vital investment that our young require.

THE ELDERLY AND THE SPECIAL CASE OF SOCIAL SECURITY

The Old-Age and Survivors Insurance (OASI) program of the social security system has revolutionized life in America, not only for the aged but also for their children and grandchildren. An overwhelming majority of Americans will receive retirement benefits from the federal government, or are already receiving them. Until the introduction and near universalization of "social security," most Americans expected to work until disability—or death—made it impossible to continue, or else hoped to survive on the largesse of their children. The elderly poor were ubiquitous.

There are still many elderly poor. But thanks in considerable part to generous social security benefits, poverty is now no more extensive among the elderly than among other age groups. To millions, though, social security benefits are virtually the sole source of income. For millions more they are a crucial foundation for supplements from private pensions and income from savings.

The Clinton fiscal 1994 budget anticipated Old-Age and

Survivors Insurance (OASI) costs, without disability payments,[7] at $283.5 billion, to which are to be added "supplemental security income" (SSI) of $27.1 billion for those who would otherwise have very low benefits. The total of $310.6 billion, some 6 percent of personal income, is a major component of the so-called entitlements, the curbing of which has been a conspicuous aim of the extreme budget and deficit cutters who have come to be known as "deficit hawks."

Major as social security retirement benefits have become and much as they have been the focus of partisan political debate, there is about as much understanding of the nature of the social security system as there is of the budget deficit. Many even fail to observe its legal requirements, as was made clear in the "nanny-gate" difficulties at the onset of the Clinton administration. But if few employers of domestic workers have, at least until recently, been making required "contributions" to social security funds, few Americans in general have any notion of the nature of these "funds" or even of what they can expect to receive from them when they retire. And certainly few understand—or have even thought about—the impact of the social security system on the overall functioning of the economy.

SOCIAL AND PRIVATE INSURANCE

The social security system mimics a private insurance system. Premiums are labeled "contributions for social insurance," not taxes. Benefits are viewed as a return, with some supplement based on devious calculations, of what retirees have paid in. They are "entitled" to these benefits because of their age and previous contributions, qualified for those under 70 by limitations as to current wage and self-employment earnings. Benefits are expected to exceed prior contributions, as they would with private annuities, on the basis of the earn-

---

[7]The total of OASDI costs, including disability insurance, was put at $321.6 billion in the 1993 Trustees Report for OASDI.

ings that might have been received if the contributions had been privately invested. In fact, until recently, benefits have generally exceeded those that might have been enjoyed for similar contributions to private pension plans. Whatever the "earnings" might have been on private investment, participants have received cost-of-living adjustments, based on the consumer price index, as prices have risen.

While, as with private insurance, contributions have gone into funds or portfolios of investments out of which payments have been made, for most of its existence social security has been run essentially on a pay-as-you-go basis. Balances have been relatively small, sufficient merely to offer a modest cushion between income and outgo so that, whatever the short-run fluctuations in cash flow, checks can be covered without resort to borrowing or subsidy from the Treasury. Since the changes enacted in 1983, the social security retirement fund balances have been growing, with the OASI fund accumulating annual surpluses estimated to come to some $63 billion in fiscal 1994. If accountants separate these surpluses as "off-budget" in the curious language dictated by Congress, the remaining accounts will show a deficit $63 billion larger than the $255 billion projected for the "unified budget" total. This has led to the charge that the true size of "the deficit" is masked by these social security surpluses.

Segregating the payroll taxes which constitute "contributions for social insurance" from other tax revenues, however, makes little economic sense. And segregating the benefits paid out from other federal outlays only adds more confusion to the social security picture. My mother used to assure me that all of the food I ate "went into the same stomach." Whatever name Congress or accountants give to Uncle Sam's levies on taxpayers, they are withdrawals from the purchasing power of the private sector. And however benefit payments may be designated, they are additions to that purchasing power. In this fundamental sense the taxes and expenditures for social security are like all other federal taxes and expenditures and, in terms of their impact on the economy, should be integrated with them.

SOCIAL SECURITY AND THE ECONOMY

The impact of the social security system on the economy has been a matter of considerable debate among economists as well as politicians. In 1964, Barry Goldwater seemed to suggest the possibility of privatizing social security. The public perception that he might "abolish social security" contributed to his landslide electoral defeat.

In the following decade, Martin Feldstein, later to become chairman of President Reagan's Council of Economic Advisers, but then (and now) a distinguished professor at Harvard University and president of the National Bureau of Economic Research, caused quite a stir with an article concluding that the social security system had reduced private saving, investment, and the U.S. private capital stock by 38 percent.[8] This reduced real growth, GNP per capita, and the standard of living by 15 percent.

Feldstein's argument was that social security had been giving people benefits in excess of their contributions and the income that might have been earned from these contributions if they had been invested privately. Understanding this, people consumed more. On the (implicit) assumption that total employment and income were givens, more consumption meant less income and output for saving and investment. Feldstein had only to employ appropriate econometric techniques to estimate the impact on consumption, with adjustment for possible changes in retirement ages, of his calculated changes in social security "net wealth" held by the public over the years, chiefly as a consequence of change in the laws.

Feldstein's conclusions were challenged in a number of professional papers, including interventions by Robert Barro,[9] who, I have noted, insists that government debt, whether explicit or implicit, has no effect on consumption. I pointed out

---

[8]Martin Feldstein, "Social Security, Induced Retirement and Aggregate Accumulation," *Journal of Political Economy,* vol. 82, September–October 1974, pp. 905–925.
[9]Among them *The Impact of Social Security on Private Savings: Evidence from the U.S. Time Series,* American Enterprise Institute, Washington, D.C., 1978.

that presumed increases in social security "debt" held by the public were generally balanced by decreases in the real value of explicit federal debt over these years. If the public had less reason to save because it could count on its "assets" in the form of government social security commitments, it had more reason to save because of its lesser real assets in the form of government savings bonds and Treasury bills, notes, and bonds. Further, the stimuli to consumption from the increase in public wealth in the form of social security commitments occurred in years when unemployment was particularly high. Increases in consumption in those times would hardly have corresponded to reductions in saving. They would have been encouraging investment rather than crowding it out.[10]

What one might have thought was the coup de grace to Feldstein's position was to be delivered, however, by two Social Security Administration economists, Dean Leimer and Selig Lesnoy,[11] who found that Feldstein's underlying calculations were in error. Feldstein acknowledged this, attributing the difficulty to a computer programming error of a graduate assistant. He later insisted, however, that with new data, his conclusions were supported!

IS SOCIAL SECURITY OVERLY GENEROUS?

More recently there have been repeated suggestions that presumably overly generous social security benefits should be pared down, in the interest of reducing the budget deficit and/or allocating federal outlays to more worthy purposes. This might be done, it has been suggested, by skipping or cutting cost-of-living adjustments or by taxing more of social security benefits. But since voting participation is clearly

---

[10] Eisner, "Social Security, Saving and Macroeconomics," *Journal of Macroeconomics*, vol. 5, no. 1, Winter 1983, pp. 1–19.
[11] Published in "Social Security and Private Saving: New Time-Series Evidence," *Journal of Political Economy*, vol. 90, June 1982, pp. 606–629.

a positive function of age, this suggestion has proved dynamite to politicians who have generally shied away from introducing such changes. Nevertheless, President Clinton in 1993 proposed increasing the social security benefits subject to taxation from 50 percent to 85 percent. This increase was to apply to those with total incomes (including 50 percent of social security benefits) over thresholds of $25,000 for individuals and $32,000 for couples, as originally proposed and approved by the House of Representatives. The Senate raised the thresholds for the proposed additional 35 percent to $32,000 for individuals and $40,000 for couples. The final legislation, apparently reflecting political concerns for the reaction of middle-class retirees, further reduced the number of taxpayers to be affected by raising the thresholds for the additional 35 percent above those in both the Senate and House versions, to $34,000 for individuals and $44,000 for couples.

This increased taxation of social security benefits threatens to aggravate an already pernicious bit of government policy. The bottom lines at which we should aim, as I have emphasized, are employment, output, and provision for the future. To those ends we should avoid policies that discourage labor and saving. Yet the law up to 1983 had exactly that effect on social security recipients, and the change, effective in 1994, makes it worse. The sticking point is what happens to effective marginal tax rates, the proportion of each dollar of *additional* earnings that is taxed.

There are objections from conservatives as well as economists in general to excessive marginal tax rates on the rich. It is argued that if the bulk of an extra dollar of income will be lost to taxes, the rich will not bother to earn it. Similarly, if the income from savings is highly taxed, people will not bother to save. I have been skeptical of both propositions. Marginal tax rates on the *taxable* income of the rich have not in recent years been high enough—28 percent for the very rich—to discourage ambitious business executives, lawyers, or doctors from working hard to maximize their income. It seems unlikely that now raising it to 39.6 percent will make much difference. More to the point, the very rich will intensify tax avoidance by taking income in the form of capital gains, tax-free interest, and sheltered investments.

HIGH EFFECTIVE MARGINAL TAX RATES
ON SOME SOCIAL SECURITY RECIPIENTS

Social security benefits are another matter. The combination of loss of benefits as labor earnings rise above thresholds for those between the ages of 62 and 69, the inclusion of up to 50 percent or the newly legislated 85 percent of benefits over a broadly defined income threshold in taxable income, and existing taxes on all income can bring some striking results, as may be noted in Table 6.1.

Social security recipients 70 years of age or older, over the minimum earnings threshold and in the 15 percent tax bracket, but without all of their benefits already subject to taxation, would keep 70 cents of each dollar of additional gross labor earnings, under pre-1994 law. This figure will shrink to 65 cents in 1994. Those in the 28 percent tax bracket would keep 50 cents under pre-1994 law and 41 cents in 1994.

For those under the age of 70, matters get complicated. If aged 65 to 69, they lose one dollar of social security benefits for every three dollars of labor earnings over an exemption which is expected to be $10,920 in 1994. However, a worker who attains age 65 in 1992 or 1993 and delays retirement—or loses benefits due to earnings—receives a "delayed retirement credit" that will raise benefits by 4 percent for each year of benefits withheld or "delayed." By the year 2009, that credit is to rise to the 8 percent per year of benefits withheld that would correspond to the actuarial value of the loss. Thus, even after offsetting the reduction for earnings with the delayed retirement credit, there is at this time a net loss, in actuarial present value, of 16.667 cents of social security benefits for each dollar of labor earnings, until labor earnings

Table 6.1   *Effective Federal Marginal Employee Tax Rates*
on Social Security Recipients for Additional
Labor Income over Thresholds*

A. 15% Tax Bracket

	Age		
	70+	*65–69*	*62–64*
Tax on Labor Income	15.0%	15.0%	15.0%
Tax on Social Security Income			
Pre-1994			
(1 or 5/6 or 3/4) × .50 × 15%	7.5%	6.3%	5.6%
Beginning 1994			
(1 or 5/6 or 3/4) × .85 × 15%	12.8%	10.6%	9.6%
Employee Social Security Payroll Tax	6.2%	6.2%	6.2%
Employee Medicare Tax	1.5%	1.5%	1.5%
Loss of Social Security Income			
With actuarial correction for			
delayed retirement credit	—	16.7%	0.0%
Without actuarial correction for			
delayed retirement credit	—	33.3%	50.0%
Total			
With actuarial correction for			
delayed retirement credit			
Pre-1994	30.2%	45.6%	28.3%
Beginning 1994	35.4%	49.9%	32.2%
Without actuarial correction for			
delayed retirement credit			
Pre-1994	30.2%	62.2%	78.3%
Beginning 1994	35.4%	66.6%	82.2%

B. 28% Tax Bracket

	Age		
	70+	*65–69*	*62–64*
Tax on Labor Income	28.0%	28.0%	28.0%
Tax on Social Security Income			
Pre-1994			
(1 or 5/6 or 3/4) × .50 × 28%	14.0%	11.7%	10.5%
Beginning 1994			
(1 or 5/6 or 3/4) × .85 × 28%	23.8%	19.8%	17.8%
Employee Social Security Payroll Tax	6.2%	6.2%	6.2%
Employee Medicare Tax	1.5%	1.5%	1.5%

Table 6.1   (*Continued*)

B. 28% Tax Bracket

	Age		
	70+	*65–69*	*62–64*
Loss of Social Security Income			
With actuarial correction for delayed retirement credit	—	16.7%	0.0%
Without actuarial correction for delayed retirement credit	—	33.3%	50.0%
Total			
With actuarial correction for delayed retirement credit			
Pre-1994	49.7%	64.0%	46.2%
Beginning 1994	59.5%	72.2%	53.5%
Without actuarial correction for delayed retirement credit			
Pre-1994	49.7%	80.7%	96.2%
Beginning 1994	59.5%	88.8%	103.5%

*The rates in this table are applicable to persons who are beyond the thresholds for taxation of benefits and reduction of benefits due to earnings, and who do not yet have benefits totally withheld for earnings or have fully 50 (85) percent of benefits subject to income taxation. All figures are rounded to tenths of a percent; the employee Medicare tax is actually 1.45 percent.

Source: Prepared by author, with help from Harry C. Ballantyne, chief actuary, and Stephen Gross of the Office of the Actuary of the Social Security Administration.

exceed the minimum threshold by three times the otherwise allowable social security benefits.[12]

If would-be workers are aged 62 to 64, they lose one dollar of benefits for every two dollars of labor earnings over the minimum threshold, which is expected to be $7,920 in 1994. There is thus an implicit tax of 50 percent on the excess of wages over the threshold up to twice otherwise allowable benefits. But for persons under age 65, the withholding of benefits under the retirement test now results in full recoupment of the benefits later, on the average, because the actuarial re-

---

[12]Those who do not expect to live as long as the actuarial forecasts can anticipate losing more; those who live longer would lose less—or even gain, if they live a very, very long time.

duction factor for early retirement (i.e., before age 65) is adjusted for the benefits not received.

All this generates a substantial set of possibilities, documented in Table 6.1. Including the current delayed retirement credits, we find effective marginal tax rates on labor earnings over the minimum thresholds, until those earnings are such that all retirement benefits have been withheld or subjected to taxation, taking into account both benefit taxation and reduction for earnings, as follows: for those 62 to 64 years of age and in the 15 percent income tax bracket, 28 percent, rounding to the nearest integer, under pre-1994 law and 32 percent beginning in 1994; for those in the 28 percent income tax bracket, these rates rise respectively to 46 percent and 53 percent. For those 65 to 69 years of age and in the 15 percent tax bracket, effective tax rates are 46 percent under pre-1994 law and 50 percent beginning in 1994; in the 28 percent tax bracket they are respectively 64 percent and 72 percent.

If delayed retirement credits are not considered, perhaps because workers are not aware of them or don't expect to live to enjoy them or have a surviving spouse who will enjoy them, results can get extreme. Those 65 to 69 years of age see a net return out of each dollar of additional labor earnings of 38 cents under the pre-1994 law and 33 cents in 1994, if in the 15 percent tax bracket, and 19 cents and 11 cents, if in the 28 percent bracket.

If those aged 62 to 64 for some reason do not take into account actuarial benefits to be received later to compensate for benefits withheld now, the results can be startling. If in the 15 percent tax bracket, they would be left with 22 cents under pre-1994 law and 18 cents beginning in 1994. And—breathe hard—if such a person aged 62 to 64 caught in the 28 percent tax bracket, and caught between the thresholds and the point of total elimination of benefits or maximum taxation of benefits, earns an extra dollar, he or she, under pre-1994 law is left with 4 cents, and beginning in 1994 is left with 3.5 cents *less* of after-tax income. His or her effective tax rate—the federal rate alone—would be 103.5 percent! And state and local income taxes, where they exist, would only make matters worse.

Saving, as well as working, is in principle discouraged by the current tax provisions for social security recipients. And it too would be somewhat more discouraged, for those over the applicable thresholds, by the proposal to raise the proportion of social security earnings subject to income taxes from 50 percent to 85 percent. Beneficiaries—and prospective beneficiaries—might reckon that saving more[13] would trigger greater taxation of retirement benefits. But since this does not trigger the loss of benefit associated with labor earnings and applies only to the earnings on accumulated savings, not the saving itself, the direct effect on saving is probably much less than the effect on labor.

REAL PROBLEMS OF THE SOCIAL SECURITY SYSTEM

Discouragement of labor, and possibly to some extent saving as well, is particularly glaring in the light of the real problems of the social security retirement system. It has little or nothing to do with the amount of the trust fund "balances," the special, non-negotiable Treasury securities held by the funds—$319 billion in the Old-Age and Survivors Insurance and Disability Insurance funds combined at the end of fiscal 1992. The OASDI balance is projected by the middle of three scenarios to reach $812 billion (1993 dollars) by 2002 and peak by about 2020, when the balance is $1,674 billion. The precariousness of these projections is indicated by the huge difference generated in the projections of the more "optimistic" scenario, which puts the balance at $1,180 billion (1993 dollars) in 2002 and $5,250 billion in 2025 and shows it continuing to rise thereafter, reaching $22,206 billion in 2070,

---

[13] In assets that generated income to be included in the total to which the threshold relates, which in this case includes tax-free interest.

the last year projected. Under the pessimistic scenario the balances would be exhausted by the year 2017.

But the securities "in" the trust funds or the computer entries listing these obligations are not what will provide real benefits to those retired and not working now or in the future. Rather, these will depend on the output of those working. The more people that are born now, the more will be working to bake the bread eaten by those not working in the year 2025. This number can and probably will be enhanced by immigration between now and then.

The more physical capital, public and private, that we accumulate between now and then, the greater output will be at that time. And, most important, the more we accumulate in human capital and the other intangible capital that comes from research and know-how, the more productive we will be in the future.

If we do not have an adequate labor force producing enough for itself and those not working, all the money in the trust funds—or all that Congress may legislate in the way of benefits—will be of little avail. If there are not enough goods and services being produced, some people, including the elderly, will come up short.

SOCIAL SECURITY FUND SURPLUSES AND "ON-BUDGET" DEFICITS

It is frequently argued that the government is using the social security trust funds to finance the deficit in the rest of the budget, "investing" them in Treasury securities instead of making productive investments in corporate bonds and stocks. It is hard to believe that those raising this supposed problem understand the nature of government finance or the *real* issues of providing for the elderly.

The social security trust funds actually have no economic significance. They are merely an accounting device to keep separate track of certain government receipts and payouts. Social security recipients could receive their checks just as regularly if no such "trust funds" existed. They will receive their checks as long as the law says they will—and the executive branch of government obeys the law.

The law currently provides that excesses of certain tax receipts for social insurance over outlays for certain classes of benefits be "invested" in government securities with interest payments credited to these accounts ("funds"). These "securities" have usually been nonmarketable and need be no more than computer entries. Whatever the entries, the excess of government receipts over payouts, if any, from these designated taxes and outlays is used elsewhere, to finance other outlays, lower other tax receipts, or reduce overall borrowing requirements. There are no other mathematical possibilities.

What else do critics think could be done? Take the excess receipts, generally in the form of checks, and use them to obtain cash from the public and the banks and put the cash in storage vaults? This would merely drain the economy of cash, and people would run to banks to get more. The banks would in turn run to their bank, the Federal Reserve, to ask for more cash. The Federal Reserve would oblige by having more Federal Reserve notes printed, with the people using the checking balances they had received from the original Social Security Fund cash acquisitions to get their cash back. If the Federal Reserve refused to offer their notes, we would learn to live with all the inconveniences of a cashless society.

We could have the trust funds use their surpluses not to acquire government securities but private bonds and mortgages and even stocks. That would leave the Treasury borrowing more from the public to finance its operations, while the funds use their surpluses to buy up the debt and equity of American (or even foreign) business. If carried far enough, and projected surpluses over some decades ahead are so large as to carry matters pretty far, this would leave us with an economy in which public ownership—by the government trust fund—would replace the private profit, private capitalist system with which we are familiar. Are advocates of using the trust funds to "invest" in other than government securities really closet socialists?

A LAST WORD ON YOUNG AND OLD
AND INTERGENERATIONAL TRANSFERS

Beware the charts of Ross Perot's United We Stand, the Rudman–Tsongas Concord Coalition, the imaginative economists who would persuade you that what is happening to the young or old depends in any direct way on public debt or deficits or the specters of awesome future tax burdens they project. Rather, what happens to young and to old will depend largely on the overall functioning of the economy. And it will depend on what we do in the way of public and private action to distribute current output and, by investment broadly defined, to affect the output to be distributed in the future. It will then depend upon private responsibility and enlightened public policy. That public policy will set an appropriate framework for private action and, where necessary, mandate proper social insurance and investment in the education and health of our people. It will permit and encourage action consistent, as far as possible, with individual preferences and principles of fairness to young and old, today and tomorrow, and those currently alive as well as those to be born in the future.

CHAPTER 7

More Misunderstandings and Myths: Money and Inflation

"The myth persists that Federal deficits create inflation and budget surpluses prevent it. . . . Obviously deficits are sometimes dangerous—and so are surpluses. But honest assessment plainly requires a more sophisticated view than the old and automatic cliché that deficits automatically bring inflation. . . . What we need is not labels and clichés but more basic discussion of the sophisticated and technical questions involved in keeping a great economic machine moving ahead."—John F. Kennedy, 1962.[1]

"Core Inflation Climbs 0.5% for 2nd Month" was the headline that appeared in the *New York Times* on March 18, 1993. Fact: *prices* rose 0.5%, not inflation. Anyone knowing the most elementary calculus would understand the difference, but it should not take that much knowledge. Inflation is itself the rate at which prices are rising. If inflation were to *rise* by 0.5 percent it would signify that the rate at which prices were rising was increasing, something economists call "accelerating inflation." Thus, if prices had risen by 0.5 percent the preceding month and now by 1.0 percent, inflation would have risen by 0.5 percent. Or, if inflation had been zero the preceding month and now was 0.5 percent, it would also have risen by 0.5 percent. Of course, what the *Times* headline—and the article—should have said is that while prices

---

[1]From Arthur M. Okun, *The Political Economy of Prosperity* (Washington, D.C.: Brookings Institution, 1970), p. 45. Quoted in James D. Savage, *Balanced Budgets and American Politics* (Ithaca and London: Cornell University Press, 1988), p. 177.

again rose 0.5 percent, inflation did not rise, but remained the same at 0.5 percent.

To some, this may seem like laboring the obvious, at least once it is explained. But it is fundamentally important to our understanding of a phenomenon that is perhaps even more misunderstood than budget deficits. Almost everyone will say he or she is against inflation. And almost none knows what he or she is talking about. Few know how inflation is measured or have any feel for the numbers. If a Gallup Poll were to ask what the rate of inflation was last year, how many would come close to the actual number of about 3 percent? If they were asked how much prices went up, on the average, each week in the last year, and given a choice of "A: hardly at all in a week," "B: about half a percent," "C: about one percent," and "D: more than 1 percent," what would be the answers? I bet that only a minority would pick the first, correct answer, although each of the others would imply enormous annual rates, of 30 percent and 67 percent for answers B and C.

IS INFLATION SO BAD?

If people don't know what inflation is or how it is measured, why will almost all of them say they are against it? "The good news," says the television commentator, is that inflation is low, or that it is expected to be low. Is that good news? Lower prices may be welcomed by buyers, but for every buyer there must be a seller. Are lower prices good for sellers?

For many years there were rapid increases in housing prices. It seemed almost impossible to lose money in housing. The question was not how much you had to pay for a house but how much more you could sell it for in a few years. High interest rates, particularly since interest payments were tax deductible, were only a modest concern for most buyers, as payments not already recouped in lesser income taxes would more than be covered in eventual sales proceeds. Housing markets and construction boomed in many areas. Even if a person did not anticipate selling a house in a few years, it seemed wise, in the face of higher prices, to buy and to buy soon, before prices went up even more.

What was true for housing was and is true in many industries. Inflation can be good for you! True, we are talking about moderate inflation and not about rapidly or continuously accelerating inflation. Clearly, if the inflation is so rapid that the very function of money comes into question, we are in serious trouble. It is hard to do business if, between the time you receive money and the time you can spend it, its value has been cut in half. But what about the kind of inflation we experience in the United States, at least in peacetime? One percent, 3 percent, 5 percent, even 10 percent per year? Does that really hurt?

Higher prices hurt buyers, but they help sellers. And inflation, it must be understood, is a *general* increase in prices, an increase in the average of all prices, including wages and salaries, the price of labor. Since for every buyer there must be a seller, there is no prima facie case that moderate inflation, in the aggregate, hurts more than it helps. If it is not anticipated, though, so that prices and wages and interest rates and people's portfolios do not adjust, some may be hurt and others helped; the distributions of income and of wealth may change, even though their totals are not affected.

SHOE LEATHER AND OTHER COSTS
OF ANTICIPATED INFLATION

Critical to evaluating the effects and costs of inflation is whether it has been anticipated, and anticipated for a long enough time, so that all wages, prices, and interest rates, as well as the forms in which people hold their assets—money, bonds, stocks, real estate, and the like—have had a chance to adjust, and continue to adjust as the inflation continues. In that case we can assume that real wages are not affected, since wages would rise as fast as prices.

Economists usually assume that interest rates will reflect

inflation expectations. Lenders and borrowers would, in principle, be concerned with real returns and real costs. Those ready to lend at, say, a 4 percent real return would want interest payments at a rate of 7 percent if prices were expected to rise at 3 percent per year. If inflation expectations rose to 5 percent, they would demand a 9 percent interest rate. Similarly, borrowers ready to meet real costs of 4 percent would pay 7 percent interest with inflation expectations of 3 percent and 9 percent with inflation expectations of 5 percent. They would reason, as might house buyers, that they would recoup the higher interest charges in the appreciation of their property.

This is the so-called Fisher effect, named for Irving Fisher, the distinguished Yale economist who enunciated it well over half a century ago. Imagine what would happen if this effect held. Borrowers and lenders would be indifferent to the rate of inflation, as would employers and employees. The economy would be quite unaffected by modest inflation, except for one factor so small that it has, perhaps derisively, been labelled "shoe-leather costs."

This refers to the possibility that we will not want to hold as much noninterest-bearing cash if inflation, expected inflation, and hence interest rates are all higher. Instead of taking $100 from an interest-bearing account for purchases over the week, we will withdraw $50 twice a week. That way we reduce our average cash holdings, on the assumption that expenditures are made evenly over the week, from $50 to $25. We will enjoy interest on the average extra $25 remaining in the account. But the cost of that interest would be the shoe leather we would wear out in an extra weekly trip to the bank or ATM.

How much that might amount to is indicated by the fact that we would hardly incur more in the way of extra shoe-leather costs than the extra interest costs brought on by the inflation. At 5 percent inflation this would come to all of .05 times the original average $50 of cash holdings in our example, or $2.50 a year. For the economy as a whole, with cash holdings of about $300 billion (much of it probably with drug dealers or other illegal operators or out of the country), this could not exceed $15 billion, or about one-quarter of 1 percent of GDP, and it would certainly be less. Clearly we will not use shoe leather to the point of holding no cash at all—nor would the drug dealers, tax dodgers, and foreigners who hold much of the $300 billion.

At this rarified theoretical level, however, there is still one other effect of modest, steady inflation (the Tobin–Mundell effect, named after James Tobin, the Keynesian Nobel laureate Yale economist, and Robert Mundell, a supply-side economist at Columbia University). This suggests that with inflation and higher nominal interest rates people will want to hold less money, so they will look for other forms of asset in which to place their wealth. Such forms could include bonds and real assets of plant and equipment, or the businesses that own them. In seeking any of these assets, people will generate more investment, as they try directly to obtain more physical assets and thus raise the value of businesses that possess physical capital or, by trying to acquire bonds and thus raising their prices, lower real interest rates and hence increase the demand for physical capital.[2]

GAINS FROM INFLATION—AND TAX ADVANTAGES . . .

In the real world, however, inflation does make more of a difference. For one thing, for whatever reason, the Fisher effect does not seem to hold, at least not fully. Higher inflation is clearly associated with higher interest rates, but the association is not one for one. When inflation rises by 5 percentage

---

[2]The higher nominal interest rates generated by the inflation raise the attractiveness of bonds versus cash. The increased demand for bonds then raises their prices, preventing nominal interest rates from rising as much as inflation, which means lowering real interest rates. The lower real interest rates then generate an increased demand for physical capital. Given the real returns from physical capital, lower real interest rates raise the present value of these returns, hence raising the demand price—what people are willing to pay for physical capital. The higher demand price brings forth a greater supply, so that the amount of physical capital in use is increased.

points, interest rates may rise by only 3 points. When inflation increases, therefore, real rates of interest tend to decline.

The lower real rates of interest raise the demand for capital and thus stimulate investment. Housing tends to boom in an inflationary period. True, mortgage interest rates will be high and make it difficult for cash-strapped buyers to make high monthly payments. But the prospect of capital gains on houses—or the fear that prices will be out of reach if they wait—lures more and more people into purchasing homes. A similar phenomenon occurs for business investment.

One reason higher rates of inflation seem to be associated with lower real interest rates is found in the tax system. Business interest costs are tax deductible while interest receipts are effectively not taxed, or not taxed fully for many kinds of investors—nonprofit institutions, pension funds, and banks (which can avoid taxes by charging interest payments and other costs against interest receipts while earning other nontaxable income). Inflation is then a heads-you-win and tails-you-do-not-lose affair. Borrowers find their interest costs due to inflation are tax deductible; lenders find their added income receipts are not taxed.

A numerical example may make this clear. Suppose a firm is paying 6 percent interest on its borrowing, with a 33 percent tax rate, under conditions of zero inflation. Its real after-tax interest cost is 4 percent. Now suppose inflation is at 6 percent and interest rates, consequently, at 6 + 6 or 12 percent. The firm's nominal after-tax interest cost is 12 percent minus the 33 percent (or one-third) reduction in taxes generated by the interest cost deduction, or 8 percent. But with 6 percent inflation its real after-tax interest cost is 8 minus 6, or 2 percent, 2 percent below the 4 percent cost in the zero inflation situation.

A nontaxable lender, however, finds the real after-tax return, which was 6 percent in the zero inflation case, now equal to 12 minus 6, still 6 percent with the 6 percent inflation. Lenders are just as willing to lend, but borrowers find the real costs of borrowing less. Inflation will thus induce borrowers to increase their demand for funds until they drive the marginal

costs of obtaining funds back to equality with the cost of supplying them. This increased borrowing will, at least in part,
be used to finance increased investment.

There is another important tax consideration. While inflation permits larger tax deductions for interest costs, returns
may be taken in the form of "unrealized" capital gains, which
are not taxable at all, or realized capital gains, of which only
the realized portions are taxable and then at reduced rates.
Taking into account that capital gains are taxable only on
"realization," which for individuals is escaped fully at death
(capital gains taxes are not paid on appreciated assets passed
on in estates), reduces the effective tax rate on capital gains
to some 4 percent or 6 percent by various estimates. Therefore, there is great advantage to borrowing at high nominal,
tax-deductible interest costs to finance the acquisition of capital on which one will enjoy gains in value taxed at a much
lower rate.[3]

Even without these tax considerations, inflation is likely
to make a difference precisely because it can never be fully
anticipated and the time it would take for a full adjustment
to a new rate may be very long. Inflation, after all, does fluc-
tuate. If, because of a change in government policy, or for any
other reason, current inflation increases, how can we be sure
that it will stay at its new higher level indefinitely? It may,
of course, go still higher—a possibility we will consider—or
it may subside. To the extent that investors operate on considerable past experience, they may generally expect that increases in inflation are at least partially temporary, not likely
to persist indefinitely. That means that interest rates cannot
be expected to rise one-for-one with actual, current inflation.

---

[3] One of the factors in this low effective tax rate, perhaps not widely perceived, is
that one can realize gains on assets without selling all of them. For example, suppose
one has 2,000 shares of stock originally selling for $50 per share, thus worth
$100,000. Now suppose the stock rises 10 percent to $55, thus increasing in total
value to $110,000. To "realize" the $10,000 gain one has only to sell off 182 shares
(precisely, 181.82 shares at $55 per share). But the gain on the shares sold is only
$5 per share times 182 or $910. The maximum tax on this, currently at 28 percent,
is $255. The effective tax rate on the gain is thus $255 \div 10,000$ or 2.55 percent!

A rise in inflation may thus put business in a position where the increase in prices they perceive for the goods they are producing is not fully offset by the higher interest costs of financing production.

Whatever the precise explanations, it appears that higher inflation has been associated with lower real interest rates, greater tax advantages, and hence more investment. Inflation has not proved "neutral" in its aggregate effects. In fact, contrary to popular views, inflation, at least of the internally generated kind, has tended to be beneficial. It has been accompanied by more investment, more production, and more employment, except when it was caused by higher external costs—for example, the huge oil price increases of the 1970s—and accompanied by repressive government policies to combat it.

If the generally moderate inflation that we have had is so benign or even beneficial, in the aggregate, why is it frequently listed high, if not at the top, in public opinion rankings of our serious economic problems? In part, this is because of the one-sided vision of many people. We treat the gains from inflation as a result of our own effort or good fortune, but blame inflation for our losses. Workers who see wages rise as part of a general increase in prices credit their productivity, their union, their company, or their government. But the associated price increases, without which their wages would not have risen, are blamed on inflation.

... AND COSTS OF INFLATION

It is also true, however, that many do suffer when inflation occurs. The fact is that inflation is not fully anticipated. All prices, wages, and interest rates do not adjust. Many people have long-term contracts. In particular, those living on relatively fixed incomes may suffer cruelly if inflation accelerates. The prices and values of their bonds fall as interest rates rise and the real value of their interest income falls. It is small comfort to those who lose that there are borrowers who gain when increases in inflation enable them to pay back in cheaper dollars than anticipated.

Those who have borrowed short and lent long, like banks and savings and loan associations, may suffer grievously from the rising interest rates that accompany increasing inflation. Their costs of funds rise as they are forced to pay higher interest rates to retain deposits, while their returns are limited by the terms of their loans of long duration. Small wonder that banks and financial institutions in general are "hawks" on inflation, usually ready to slow the economy and brook substantial unemployment to ensure against increases in inflation! One may wonder, however, how much their self-interest should be allowed to influence policy for the economy as a whole.

INFLATION CAN RAISE YOUR TAXES

I have noted certain tax advantages afforded by inflation. There are some penalties, particularly in the area of *realized* capital gains and depreciation. In the case of the former, taxpayers pay on gains that are not real. Effective tax rates on the real gains can be enormous, to the point of taxing the capital itself; the effective rate may be more than 100 percent. Suppose, for example, a farmer has a piece of land that he bought 10 years ago for $200,000 and sells now for $300,000. He pays a tax (at most, according to tax laws in effect in 1993) of $28,000 on his nominal capital gain of $100,000. But suppose, further, that the general level of prices rose by 40 percent over this period so that he would have had to realize $280,000 to get back the real value of his original purchase. The farmer's real capital gain is only $20,000, on which he has paid a tax of $28,000, an effective rate of taxation of 140 percent.

The farmer can, of course, avoid this tax by not "realizing" his gain. He can borrow against his farm if he needs cash or possibly work out a lease arrangement with a purchaser that will delay or avoid the legal sale and the "realization" that triggers the tax. Or he can try to offset his gain with other losses or find other means of avoiding the tax. But there is no doubt that inflation causes problems with the current system of taxes on capital gains, and heavy effective taxes for those forced to "realize" their gains.

The situation with regard to depreciation is analogous. Depreciation charges for tax purposes are calculated on the original cost of assets. In periods of inflation, the cost of replacing these assets when they wear out or become obsolete may well be more than their original cost. Taxes are presumably levied on earnings net of depreciation. If allowable deductions for depreciation are less than replacement costs, the effective tax on the true net earnings is higher than its nominal rate.

Again a numerical example may make this clear. A firm may have gross earnings of $200 million and allowable depreciation charges of $100 million. Therefore, it pays a tax, say, of 36 percent on its $100 million of taxable income, or $36 million. But with the increase in prices of assets since their acquisition averaging, say, 50 percent, "economic depreciation," reflecting this inflation and the increased cost of replacing expiring assets, would be $150 million. The firm's true net income is then really only $200 million minus $150 million, or $50 million. The $36 million tax is 72 percent of its income!

In general, firms are compensated for this by being allowed to depreciate property for tax purposes in more or less accelerated fashion. Accelerated depreciation means that depreciation charges are higher on assets when they are new and less when they are old. In growing firms—and firms are more generally growing than not—recent acquisitions will be greater than older acquisitions. Inflation makes the value of recent acquisitions, in comparison with older ones purchased at lower prices, all the greater, but adds still more to replacement costs, which are based on current prices. Since acceleration of depreciation concentrates the depreciation on these more recent, higher-valued property additions, it generates greater total depreciation charges. If inflation is moderate, the shortage of allowable depreciation deductions resulting from higher replacement costs is roughly offset by the excess depreciation resulting from the acceleration. If inflation is low, the accelerated depreciation allowances tend to be excessive, thus effectively shielding real net income from taxation. But when inflation is high, greater than the rate of real growth of property additions, say, over 4 percent, the effective rate of taxation tends to be raised above the nominal rate. Higher inflation then does raise taxes more than the acceleration of depreciation lowers them.

CHANGING THE RULES IN THE MIDDLE OF THE GAME

Beyond the fact that changes in inflation bring winners and losers, many people have a sense there is something inherently unfair about inflation. As we try to "play by the rules," we base our economic decisions on sets of prices, and changes in prices, which we assume are not capricious. It doesn't seem right to shuffle the deck and redistribute real income and wealth on a new basis. Nor does it seem right to give extra rewards, at the expense of the rest of us, to those who can take advantage of changes in the rules.

This caveat is less applicable to inflation itself, however, than to changes in the rate of inflation. With a steady but modest rate of inflation—say 3 percent per year—the economy adjusts. Lenders get repaid in cheaper dollars but in more of them, as nominal interest rates are higher. Wage earners find their stipends going up 3 percent per year faster and their real wages are preserved. While costs are rising 3 percent per year more, so are prices; hence profits rise at the same 3 percent. Savers learn to put their money into assets that rise with inflation or pay the higher interest rates associated with the inflation. Government adjusts social security benefits and employee pensions to the cost of living.

Some of the innocent or ignorant or helpless may fail to take assets out of cash under the mattress or anything else that is a real inflation loser, and there are tax complications that I have pointed out. But the general view is that when we have gotten used to modest inflation and learned to anticipate it, the move from a regime of stable prices introduces little inequity.

Changes in the rate of inflation, however, are another matter. An increase in inflation, by raising nominal interest rates, can lead to falls in bond prices and impose serious losses on lenders. For that matter, a fall in the rate of inflation can impose serious losses on long-term borrowers, who will be stuck with high interest costs while new borrowers take advantage of the lower rates. Those who bought property in anticipation of much higher prices may find it impossible to sell when the end of such anticipations takes away a major part of the property's appeal. And with changing rates of inflation, all wages and prices may well not move together. Those who by foresight or luck obtain title to goods or securities rising more rapidly in price may make a killing, while others caught by the squeeze of costs rising faster than returns may be driven to bankruptcy.

Even if changes in the rate of inflation (in either direction) do not necessarily make the overall economy worse off—although they may, certainly if bankruptcies force losers out of business—they may well introduce significant changes in the distribution of claims to income and wealth. Some people may get richer, while others suffer. And that does, understandably, strike people as an unfair change of the rules in the middle of the game.

It must be recognized, however, that all of this discussion relates to "moderate inflation," even up to the 10 percent or 12 percent annual rate we suffered at the beginning of the 1980s. Rapid, runaway inflation, or hyperinflation, would be another matter. That clearly can do considerable damage by making currency an inadequate medium of transactions as well as an impossible store of value. The very workings of a complicated, intradependent economy break down.

THE ROLE OF MONEY

"Inflation is always a monetary phenomenon!" So argued Milton Friedman, the great, Nobel laureate, conservative, monetarist economist. But is it? Does nothing else matter? Does the quantity of money have to rise to cause inflation, and does it have to rise more rapidly to bring more inflation? Can there be inflation even if the quantity of money does not increase? Just what is "money" or "the quantity of money"?

The essential argument is that we must use money to buy goods and money is held in order to be available to purchase goods. If there is a shortage of money, sellers will have to lower prices to find buyers. If we have more money than we feel any need to hold, we try to get rid of the "excess" by using it to buy more goods. Then, *if the amount of goods available cannot be increased,* efforts to buy more can only result in higher prices. Prices will rise until we no longer feel we have excess money, that is, until prices have risen proportionately with the quantity of money; thus, our *real* holdings of money are back where they were. If the money supply keeps rising at a faster rate, prices must rise at a correspondingly faster rate as we keep our real holdings of money constant.

THE MANY COLORS OF MONEY

Is the money supply a single entity controlled by the Treasury or the Federal Reserve? Or is it something multidimensional, or like the different colors of the spectrum, many not even visible to the human eye? And is it responsive not so much to the monetary authority as to other fundamental forces and movements in the economy?

The man in the street may sometimes think of money as cash or currency. But this amounts to only about $300 billion and is really little more than the small change of what we use to buy a gross domestic product that totals more than 20 times that sum in a year, or to finance transactions of all kinds, which come to much more. The great bulk of our purchases or spending—the new car or house, the rent, the college tuition, the airline ticket to romantic places—are paid for by check or credit card.[4]

---

[4]Just what those $300 billion of currency are doing or where they are is an interesting question. Dividing that figure by the U.S. population of 260 million indicates that the average or per capita cash holdings of the nation's men, women, and chil-

Broader measures of money are thus regarded as having more to do with spending and prices and inflation. One measure, seemingly closest to actual purchases, is the total of currency, a small amount of traveler's checks, and relatively large amounts of demand deposits and "other checkable deposits," not only in commercial banks but also in all kinds of "depository institutions," including savings banks, savings and loan associations, and credit unions. This total, labelled "M1," amounts now to just over one trillion dollars.

There are undoubtedly some monetarists who still view inflation as a direct response, pure and simple, to increases in "money," somehow defined, relative to output. But over the short run—a short run of a number of years—movements of money and prices have diverged considerably. In the Great Depression of the 1930s, for example, the quantity of money fell but the ratio of money to output rose, while prices fell substantially.

Over long periods, the relationship has also broken down, as may be noted in Figure 7.1. The original most highly regarded measure of money, the old M1—the total of cash outside banks and demand deposits, before there was such a thing as "other checkable deposits"—got so far out of line with growing output and rising prices that it became almost obsolete as an analytical measure or an instrument of policy. This had serious implications since it was the amount of this M1 that the Federal Reserve was supposed to seem reasonably able to determine. It did so through the system of reserve

---

dren, including infants, is about $1,150. That would suggest the preposterous result that a typical family of four might possess $4,600 in cash!

The more likely possibility is that the great bulk of these greenbacks, from dollar bills to hundreds, is to be found in several places that have little to do with the main functioning of the U.S. economy. One is the hot hands of foreigners in countries like Russia, where the domestic currency is rapidly losing its value and for many purposes seems virtually worthless. Another is with drug dealers and others who do not want to leave a paper trail. And a third is with those engaged in legal activities but securing payment in cash, which helps them avoid taxes on these activities, whether painting houses, domestic work, waiting on tables, or driving taxis. Some economists have sought to take the use of cash as a measure of the "underground" economy and the unreported if not illegal economy, and have come up with very considerable estimates of its extent.

Figure 7.1 *Changes in Prices and the Money Supply, 1930–1992*

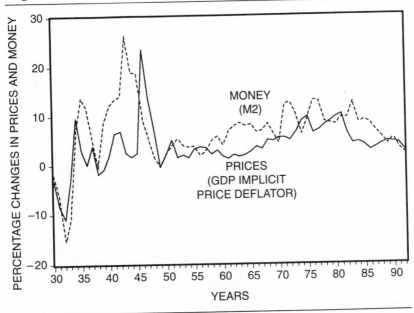

Source: GDP implicit price deflator and M2 from Robert J. Gordon, *Macroeconomics,* 6th ed. (New York; HarperCollins, 1993), Table A-1, pp. A2–A3. M2 series are averages of quarterly figures.

requirements against deposits, where it set the requirements and, through "open market operations," largely controlled the reserves.[5]

---

[5]Those who took a course in money and banking in college—and remember it—will recall that in our system money is created when banks buy assets from the nonbank public. This generally begins with the Federal Reserve buying government securities. The sellers of the securities in effect deposit their checks from the Federal Reserve and thus have money in place of government securities. Except to the extent that they may have sold the securities at a slight profit, they are no richer, but the quantity of money is higher by the amount of their sales—the Federal Reserve purchases.

There is usually a further effect. Banks in which the Federal Reserve checks have been deposited in turn deposit these checks in their banks, which are Federal Reserve banks. These balances count as reserves which enable them to buy additional securities or make additional loans. As they do so they give additional deposits to the sellers of the securities or the borrowers who give the banks their IOUs, increasing the quantity of money further.

THE CHANGING COLORS OF MONEY

Partly no doubt in response to efforts by the monetary authority to hold down the growth of M1 in its fight against inflation, new financial instruments were developed. Lacking the reserves to make loans that created more reserve-requiring demand deposits, banks and other depository institutions solicited all manner of time deposits, which required little or nothing in the way of reserves controlled by the Fed. These time deposits, including more than half a trillion dollars in essentially checkable money market funds created by brokerage houses and other nonbank institutions, dominated the narrow M1 measure. Economists and policy makers look-

---

We have, however, a fractional required reserve system, by which depository institutions must have, for roughly every eight dollars of demand and other checkable deposits, one dollar in the form of currency on hand or on deposit in their Federal Reserve banks. Each extra dollar of reserves created when the Fed buys securities in the open market thus permits depository institutions to make loans or buy additional securities such that these deposits, the major element in M1, rise by eight dollars. The depository institutions will certainly take almost full advantage of this opportunity because they earn interest and profits on all of these additional loans and securities. If the Fed sells securities in the open market, however, depository institutions are forced to scramble and reduce their loans and holdings of securities until their deposit liabilities subject to the reserve requirements have fallen eight dollars for each dollar loss of reserves. All of this then permits the Fed to have a substantial control over the quantity and growth (or decline) in the supply of M1, the major components of which are subject to these requirements. But it leaves them with little control over other broader measures of the money supply, such as M2.

Indeed, as I point out in the text, the Fed's efforts to curtail M1 may actually bring about an increase in M2 as financial institutions are driven to acquire funds for lending in forms, such as money market accounts, with little or no legal reserve requirements. A huge expansion of credit and what to all intents and purposes serves as money may then become possible on the foundation of the relatively small base of reserves that the lending institutions find it necessary or prudent to keep on their own.

Increases in the quantity of money, it should be noted, involve people or businesses having additional money in the form of bank deposits or other assets such as money market fund balances that do not represent increases in their net worth. Each additional private monetary asset is matched by an additional private liability, or a reduction in assets of government securities. And as banks or other depository institutions create more money with their lending, the monetary assets they create are matched by the increases in debt of their borrowers. Changes in the quantity of money, as they occur in our system, thus have only a small direct effect, if any (to the extent changes in interest rates change the market value of existing government securities), on people's net worth or wealth. Of course, if increases in the quantity of money lead to increased production and real investment, wealth does increase.

ing to gauge the money supply came to rely on "M2," a more comprehensive measure of money, including money market funds, savings and small time deposits, and more esoteric (to laymen at least) instruments such as repurchase agreements (RPs) and Eurodollars. In 1993 these totalled about $2.5 trillion, a far cry from the $300 billion in currency or the even smaller $55 billion in reserves required by the Fed. And these larger totals, too, drift in manners only distantly related to price movements, as may be noted in Figure 7.1.

If most monetarists (Beryl Sprinkel, the last chairman of President Reagan's Council of Economic Advisers, for example) admit to being stumped by all of this, the rest of us may have less reason to be perplexed. To begin, we view prices as determined by the relation between spending or purchases and output or the amount available for purchase. The quantity of money is only one uncertain determinant of how much we spend. More general and fundamental determinants are income and wealth and propensities to spend as consumers and invest as businesses, the last being particularly affected by rates of interest.[6] We may be just as ready to spend if we have a million dollars worth of readily marketable government obligations in the form of interest-bearing securities, which, however readily cashable, are not classified as

---

[6]Striking recognition of this has finally come from the Federal Reserve itself. As reported in the *New York Times,* July 23, 1993, in an article by Steven Greenhouse, datelined July 22:

> The Federal Reserve said today that the main yardstick it used in guiding the economy's growth for more than 15 years had become so unreliable that it would largely abandon it.
> Alan Greenspan, the central bank's chairman, said the Federal Reserve would stop relying on growth in the money supply—its traditional tool—and begin relying on interest rates, an approach more akin to the way it worked before it started relying on the money supply figures.
> In an appearance before the Senate Banking Committee today, Mr. Greenspan said the central bank was jettisoning the money supply approach because changes in the way Americans invest their money meant it could no longer predict how much economic growth would be produced by a certain amount of growth in the money supply.
> "The relationship has completely broken down," Greenspan said.

"money," as we are if we have a million dollars of private bank obligations called money.[7]

But that means that a budget deficit, which increases our wealth in the form of these government obligations, may increase our spending as much as or more than an increase in money. The latter indeed may not increase our wealth at all. As I have noted, it may, and probably does, entail only a portfolio shift as we hold more money and hold less in the way of interest-bearing securities or owe more to banks and other depository institutions.

MONEY ON AUTOPILOT

Almost half a century ago, a younger, if already brilliant, Milton Friedman married money and deficits in "A Monetary and Fiscal Framework for Economic Stability."[8] He suggested an economy in which a preset schedule of taxes and transfer payments and the government expenditures on goods and services that society considered necessary would generate a modest budget deficit to be financed not by borrowing but by the printing of additional money. The budget would be such that, at full or reasonably full employment, the deficit would generate a growth in the money supply just sufficient to accommodate the rate of growth of output expected from growth in the labor force and increases in productivity.

If, for some reason, the economy slipped and output declined and unemployment increased, the deficit would increase and

---

[7]Unless, again, we are believers in "Ricardian equivalence," convinced that any tendency for holders of government interest-bearing securities to spend more will be balanced by an equal tendency to spend less on the part of those feeling that they, or their descendants, will have to pay more in taxes in the future to service the government debt incurred by the failure to levy sufficient taxes in the present.

Since money adds more to liquidity than interest-bearing securities, even those of the Treasury, if we take monetary policy as otherwise given, the addition of one million dollars to wealth in the form of money may in fact be expected to stimulate more spending than one million dollars more in securities.

[8]*American Economic Review*, vol. 38 (June 1948), pp. 245–264. Reprinted in Milton Friedman, *Essays in Positive Economics* (Chicago: University of Chicago Press, 1953).

the money supply would grow more rapidly. If wages and prices were reasonably flexible, the slow economy would bring down prices so that the real increase in the quantity of money would be all the greater. The real quantity of money would keep growing faster than output and prices until it became great enough to turn the economy around. People with all the extra money would spend more and keep spending more until prices and output were back on their stable, high-employment path.

If the economy became overheated and inflation developed, tax revenues would rise and the small equilibrium budget deficit would change to a surplus. Money would be drained from the economy and spending would be forced down, ending the inflation and overheating. Friedman thus had proposed a program of government policies—actually a mechanism— designed to keep the economy on an even keel and prevent inflation. In good libertarian or free-market fashion, the program, once initiated, was "untouched by human hands." It was automatic, calling for no "discretionary" action by politicians or Federal Reserve bankers. And money would play a major role because in Friedman's system—unlike in the real world of our Federal Reserve system and bank creation of money—changes in the quantity of money would constitute changes in private wealth.

In his very influential presidential address to the American Economic Association two decades later,[9] Friedman again saw the role of money, at least in the long run, as affecting only prices and inflation. The economy was bound by its "natural" rates of interest and, as I shall consider in Chapter 8, unemployment. Increases in the rate of growth of the money supply would generate increases in inflation and expected inflation. Thus, while they might very temporarily lower interest rates and stimulate the economy, interest rates would quickly rise to reflect the increased expected inflation. Real interest rates would settle back at their original level and we would be left

---

[9]"The Role of Monetary Policy," *American Economic Review*, vol. 58, March 1968, pp. 1–17.

with nothing but more inflation and higher nominal interest rates.

All this, we shall find, depends critically on the notion that real output cannot be affected by what people spend. It is impervious to changes in the money supply or other factors affecting the demand for the nation's goods and services. If the economy were always at its "natural" rate of employment or unemployment, the output path would be fixed. Changes in money would then have no real effects.

A BROADER VIEW OF MONEY—
AND WHAT REALLY COUNTS

If we increase spending by 10 percent and output stays the same, it is clear that prices must have risen by 10 percent. But output may rise anywhere from zero to the full 10 percent. Then prices may rise by anywhere from 10 percent to zero. The failure of so many to realize or acknowledge this may be traced to their fixation with the idea that our fine economy is generally, if not always, in a state of full or natural employment. If employment does not vary in response to changes in spending, then output cannot vary either. In that situation a 10 percent increase in spending must be accompanied by a 10 percent rise in prices.

Let us leave Milton Friedman's old world of money on autopilot, where changes in the quantity of money represent changes in private wealth. Let us also leave a world which assumes that employment and output are fixed by natural forces beyond the influence of the monetary authority. Let us reenter the real world, in which employment and output, as well as prices, do vary, and changes in the quantity of money essentially entail exchanges of money for other obligations, such as are accomplished by Federal Reserve open-market operations and borrowing and lending by private financial institutions.

In this real world, what will happen if Alan Greenspan persuades a majority of his eleven associates on the Open

Market Committee[10] to try to increase the rate of growth of the money supply and thus ease the terms of credit? Eschewing the various subtle and esoteric tools at their command, let us assume that the word goes out to buy Treasury securities, both short-term bills and longer-term notes and bonds. As with any other securities, increased orders to buy Treasury securities bid up their prices. Recall that that means a lowering of interest rates, as securities offering the same cash return now cost more.

For rates of interest on longer-term securities to fall more than trivially, however—and these longer-term rates of interest are most relevant to business investment in plant and equipment and household borrowing to buy new houses—investors have to be convinced that the Fed will not reverse itself soon and sell securities, perhaps in a new struggle against inflation. To the extent the Fed's new policy of expansion is taken as credible and lasting, we can expect some fall in interest rates along with an increase at least in M1, that component of the money supply substantially affected by Fed creation of reserves.

The lower rates of interest can be expected to lead businesses, households, nonprofit institutions, and state and local governments, balancing costs and benefits or opportunities for profits, to find the scale tilted in favor of more investment (and also encourage individuals to borrow to buy automobiles and other durable goods). If resources are available to produce more investment goods—factories, new machinery, shopping centers, office buildings, and houses—and if decision makers think there will be a demand to purchase these capital goods or the goods and services they would produce, they will be ordered. With the increased incomes generated by the production of these additional capital goods, consumption expenditures are likely to rise as well. If resources are available to produce more consumption goods and services, people will

---

[10] Which consists of the seven members of the Board of Governors of the Federal Reserve system and five, on a partially rotating basis, of the twelve Federal Reserve Bank presidents.

treat themselves to more automobiles, more trips to the movies, more meals in restaurants, more clothing, and more travel to exotic places.

What about that bugaboo of inflation? If resources are not available to produce more, attempts to buy more will not be able to generate more production either of investment goods or consumption goods. Prices will rise and we may have a cycle of price increases and more inflation. If the economy is already booming and resources for real expansion are limited, the stimulus of the lower interest rates may bring only limited increase in investment and consumption and be largely but still not completely dissipated in higher prices and inflation.

Only in the case of full utilization of resources, full employment, or employment somehow constrained by nature will it be impossible for the monetary stimulus to generate more output; hence, it will be *entirely* dissipated in higher prices and inflation. If investors know that this is the case—or think they know because they think the economy cannot expand— the Fed's very attempt to increase the quantity of money will be recognized as inflationary. Prices will rise immediately in anticipation of the inevitable consequences. These additional price increases will correspond to more inflation and, in turn, anticipated inflation. Hence nominal interest rates will rise, to cover this inflation, not fall; real interest rates will, as a first approximation, stay the same. All the Fed—and the rest of us—will have gotten for our pains is more inflation. What really counts—employment, output, current consumption, and saving and investment for the future—will be unaffected.

How much good monetary stimulus can do in a slack economy is subject to debate, and I am not as optimistic as some; my reserve should have been clear in Chapter 3 when I discussed the possible role of the interest rate mechanism in counteracting the demand depressant of deficit reduction. But that it can do some good, and that we should try to use it for what good we can, should clearly follow from this analysis, unless we are trapped by the dogma that employment and output are fixed at their "natural" rates.

It is this assumption that rates of employment and output cannot be affected by public policy—and even that they are, in some sense, optimum and hence to be left alone—that should be most fundamentally questioned. By now, the reader should recognize that questioning it has been a central theme of this work. I shall tackle it head-on in Chapter 8.

CHAPTER 8

The Greatest Misconception of All: Natural Unemployment

"I was very concerned in 1976 about the high Federal Government deficit. When I ran for president, the Federal deficit was over $66 billion. I've not been in office yet 2 years, but the Congress and I together have already reduced the deficit by $25 billion. I'm now preparing the 1980 fiscal year budget. I'm going to cut the Federal deficit to less than half what it was when I was elected."—Jimmy Carter, 1978.[1]

"The Republican party no longer worships at the altar of a balanced budget."—Congressman Jack Kemp, testimony before the House Budget Committee, 1981.[2]

"It commits to what Ronald Reagan promised in 1981— to balance the budget."—Senator Phil Gramm, on the Gramm–Rudman–Hollings balanced budget legislation.[3]

Not many of the general public have heard of it. But for many economists in the 1970s and 1980s it seemed to be the ultimate argument against efforts to achieve full employment. It was the "natural rate" hypothesis and its companion, the nonaccelerating-inflation-rate of unemployment.

Perhaps there is good reason after all for economics to be

---

[1] From *Public Papers of the Presidents of the United States: Jimmy Carter, 1978* (Washington D.C.: USGPO, 1979), vol. 2, p. 1894. Quoted in James D. Savage, *Balanced Budgets and American Politics* (Ithaca and London: Cornell University Press, 1988), p. 191.
[2] Cited in Savage, *Balanced Budgets and American Politics*, p. 198.
[3] Ibid.

known as the dismal science. Great numbers of its practitioners in the 1970s and 1980s again accepted the notion that like poverty and a degree of economic misery, a significant amount of unemployment always had to exist. The layman should understand that economists have always recognized the fact that not everyone is expected to work. Clearly the very young and very old will not be willing and able. Allowance is also made for those who, in the pursuit of higher education, in the interest of child care, in preference for idleness, or what have you, do not wish to engage in market work. Finally, allowance is made for those "frictionally unemployed" or "voluntarily" out of work while looking for a better job.[4]

But what few economists were able to forget, at least from the Great Depression of the 1930s onward, is that there could be millions more—perhaps 25 percent of the labor force—who wanted to work but had no jobs. It was recognized that this unemployment was the result of a breakdown in the system, an inadequate "aggregate demand" or purchasing power to buy all that would have been produced if everybody had been working. And that, not nature or the need to avoid inflation, was why they were not working.

This explanation of the mass unemployment of the Great Depression received the most solid real-life confirmation when unemployment tumbled—in the United States and other nations—to a trivial 1.2 percent because of the enormous amount of government purchases during World War II. And for decades thereafter, adequate aggregate demand was seen as the key to "full employment," or a rate of unemploy-

---

[4]Academic economists almost always have another job lined up before they quit the one they have. They see no need and are not forced to go jobless while they search for new employment. Many of them, nevertheless, presume that this is the natural order of things for other workers, at least of the blue-collar variety, whom unemployment generally strikes more frequently.

Considerable unemployment is reported among the young, new entrants into the labor force, and those reentering the civilian labor force after military service or child care. This unemployment may be viewed as frictional, but it is hard to see how it is voluntary or in any sense "natural" or necessary to hold down inflation. A successful full-employment policy would surely reduce such unemployment to a minimum.

ment reduced to the voluntary or frictional, widely taken in the postwar period to be about 4 percent of the labor force.

In the immediate postwar period even conservatives such as Milton Friedman, as noted in the previous chapter, agreed that government had a role in setting up a monetary and fiscal system that would help provide the demand or purchasing power necessary to maximize or at least stabilize employment. Herbert Stein, later chairman of Richard Nixon's Council of Economic Advisers, in his capacity as chief economist of the business-sponsored Committee for Economic Development, helped ensure that old dogmas did not stand in the way of government policies directed toward high employment.

Among these dogmas were those that warned incessantly that any efforts to promote higher employment, through easier money, more government spending, or lower taxes, would be inflationary. The counterargument, which largely carried the day, was that while an increase in demand might bring some increase in prices here and there, there was little to fear in the way of major or excessive inflation until the economy neared or actually reached full utilization of its resources, that is, the full employment conservatively taken—given the war experience—at the 4 percent unemployment rate I have cited.

THE FAMOUS PHILLIPS CURVE

The devastating counterrevolution to this line of thought developed as a reaction to the "Phillips Curve," named for its discoverer, A. W. (Bill) Phillips, the late eminent economist of New Zealand origin, who did his major work at the London School of Economics. In the 1950s, Phillips analyzed some new data on wages and prices over a century of British history and came up with a relationship that set economists the world over to replicating, puzzling, and explaining. Phillips found that when unemployment was low, wages tended to go up. When unemployment got very low,

wages went up rapidly. When unemployment was high, however, wages went down very little if at all.

But wage changes were reflected in price changes, except
for the mediation of changes in productivity. There is in fact
an exact relation between the rate of wage change, $\dot{w}$, the
rate of productivity change, $\dot{\pi}$, and the rate of price change
or inflation, $\dot{p}$. This relation could be written $\dot{p} = \dot{w} - \dot{\pi}$; price
inflation equals wage inflation minus the rate of increase of
labor productivity.[5] With a constant rate of increase of productivity, say 2 percent per labor-hour annually, inflation would
always be 2 percent less than the rate of increase of wages.

Phillips noted something extraordinary. The shape of the
curve relating wage increases (or inflation) to the rate of unemployment was not linear, that is, not a straight line. The
curve was much steeper at very low rates of unemployment,
but almost horizontal with high unemployment, as illustrated
in Figure 8.1. In fact, it appeared that as unemployment got
very low, the curve approached the vertical. Even the slight-
est further reduction in unemployment would then be associated with an enormous increase in inflation. As a consequence
of this nonlinearity, an economy with sharply fluctuating unemployment seemed likely to have higher inflation than one
with the same average but less variability in unemployment.[6]

Economists scrambled to look at data in other countries,
the United States, Germany, and France in particular, and
they discovered very similar phenomena. Lower unemployment was associated with greater inflation and the trade-off

---

[5] The dots above letters are conventional mathematical symbols denoting time derivatives, that is, rates of change per unit of time. With the lowercase letters taken to
denote logarithms of the variables, we have logarithmic time derivatives, which may
be viewed as percentage changes per unit of time.

[6] Assume the Phillips Curve indicates the following relationship between unemployment and inflation: 4 percent unemployment gives 11 percent inflation; 7 percent
unemployment gives 2 percent inflation; 10 percent unemployment gives falling
prices or minus 1 percent inflation. Then an economy that always had 7 percent
unemployment would always have a modest 2 percent inflation. An economy that
passed one-third of its time in each state of unemployment would have the same
average unemployment—$(10 + 7 + 4) \div 3 = 7$—but its average inflation would
be $(11 + 2 - 1) \div 3 = 4$ percent, or twice as much inflation as the constant
unemployment economy.

Figure 8.1   *Phillips Curve*

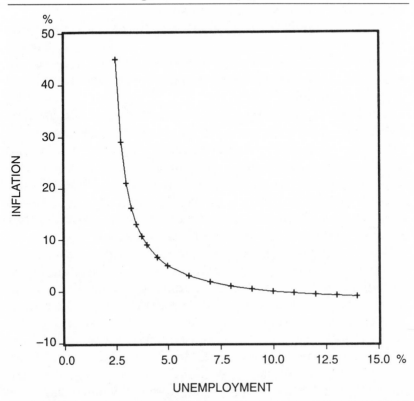

Source: Theoretical curve, by construction.

became very steep for very low unemployment. Karl Marx might have said, "I told you so! Substantial unemployment is a curse of the capitalist system, without which it cannot survive." He argued that it took a "reserve army of the unemployed" to keep wages from rising to a point where they would deprive employers of critical profits. With many outside the factory gate looking for work, the boss could easily resist upward wage pressures and did.

I have often suspected that the reluctance of much of the business community to support measures to combat unemployment stems from a tacit agreement with Marx. When unemployment is low, workers get too uppity, and it becomes difficult to keep wages and costs down.

The more sophisticated and rigorous modern explanations were not all that different. Tight labor markets—a scarcity of job seekers relative to the number of openings—drove wages up. Prospective employers had to bid higher and higher to get the workers they wanted.

Whatever the theoretical explanation, these findings indicated that while inflation itself might not reduce unemployment, the forces of increasing aggregate demand would tend to raise output and employment but, more or less simultaneously, raise prices and inflation as well. And this laid the groundwork for a political battle that still continues. How much do we want to stimulate the economy to increase output and employment if the cost is greater inflation?

I may offer some suggestions about the nature of the lineup. Bankers will opt for more unemployment and less inflation. So will the political parties (Republicans, Tories?) that identify with financial interests and those, particularly the retired elderly, who are no longer concerned with maintaining jobs. Those representing workers, particularly blue-collar workers whose employment is least stable (Democrats, Labor?) are most ready to stimulate the economy with government spending, budget deficits, and easy money, and play down warnings that such stimulation may be inflationary.

BREAKDOWN OF THE PHILLIPS CURVE—
AND THE LONG RUN

The awesome Phillips Curve, which might well have earned its discoverer a Nobel Prize if he had lived longer, broke down with a vengeance in the 1970s, a time of more inflation and *more* unemployment. With inflation on the graph's vertical axis and unemployment on the horizontal one, the curve had been sloping down from left to right. Now, if the Phillips Curve had any clear shape, it was sloping *up* from left to right. The confusing picture shown in Figures 8.2A and 8.2B is a far cry from the neat curve of Figure 8.1.

Figure 8.2A   *Actual Inflation and Unemployment
in the United States, 1947–1992*

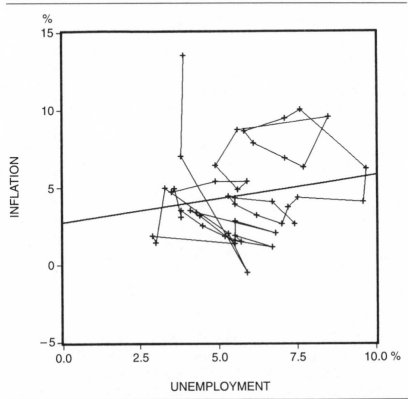

*Source: Economic Report of the President, 1993, Table B-3, pp. 352–353; Survey of
Current Business, June 1993, Table 7.1, p. 15.*

What is more, there were a couple of eminent economists
who were able to say, à la Marx previously, "I told you so!"
These were Edmund S. (Ned) Phelps of Columbia University
and, independently, our brilliant and influential defender of
free markets, Milton Friedman, then at the University of Chicago. Their argument was that there was essentially no long-
run Phillips Curve at all. The whole phenomenon was at most
a temporary, short-run one.

The inflation brought on by economic stimulus, they argued, would increase employment temporarily for one or both

Figure 8.2B   *Actual Inflation and Unemployment
in the United States, 1947–1992*

Source: See Figure 8.2A.

of two reasons. First, potential workers, seeing wage offers rise, would accept jobs that they resisted before the increase in wages. They would not realize at first that prices were or would be rising too. (Recall the wage-price relation described above.) But later they would discover that prices had risen along with nominal wages and that their real wages were no higher than when they had been deemed too low to justify taking the job. They would then quit, so that unemployment, as we measure it, would be back where it had been. We would have had no lasting reduction in unemployment, but we would still have higher prices.

The argument is put in terms of inflation, the rate of change of prices, rather than prices themselves, by explicitly including expectations of price changes. Workers respond to wage inflation along a given Phillips Curve because an increase in wage inflation is initially associated with a given expectation of price increases. The greater wage inflation makes jobs look more attractive, given that initial expectation of the extent to which future prices will be higher. But the greater wage inflation generates greater price inflation and, as workers observe this, *expectations* of greater price inflation. The higher expected wages no longer justify the increased employment. Workers again quit their jobs and we still have the same unemployment but higher inflation.

There is a second explanation, in terms of employer reactions. This argument indicates that in fact prices rise first in response to increased demand such as might be generated by higher government spending, bigger budget deficits, or an increased supply of money. As firms try to produce more to meet the greater demand at higher prices, they look for more workers. Wages go up, but later or more slowly than prices. Employers realize that their real wage costs are less because wages have not gone up as much as the prices of their products, and so hire more people. But workers, who do not shop every day everywhere, do not realize that prices have in fact already risen more than wages. Therefore, *thinking* that their real wages are *higher,* they accept additional employment. Again, however, they ultimately face reality and employers eventually find that wages, or wage increases, have risen as much as prices. Employers, faced with the same real wage costs as initially, cut production and offers of employment back to their original levels, just as workers, in the face of the original, low real wages, reduce their demand for jobs.

But Friedman, in particular, put a very powerful, provocative twist on the argument. Lower unemployment would come with higher inflation only until inflation expectations had caught up with the increase in inflation. Then unemployment would return to its original level and we would still have higher inflation. To force unemployment down again, we would have to raise inflation another notch, above the higher anticipated inflation which had caught up to the previous rate of actual inflation. It was only by keeping wage inflation greater than inflation expectations that we could enjoy more employment and less unemployment. Since experience of increased inflation would increase expectations of future inflation, expectations would keep catching up. We would thus have to keep *increasing* inflation to hold down unemployment.

Indeed, eventually, everyone would learn that our foolish policy makers were perpetually increasing inflation and expectations would adjust without delay. We would no longer have even a temporary gap between actual wage and price inflation and expectations of future inflation. The motive and the force for increased employment would disappear. As long as the government persisted in trying to stimulate the economy, inflation would accelerate, but unemployment would not change. The long-run Phillips Curve would become a vertical line in which there was no trade-off between unemployment and inflation. As long as we *tried* to reduce unemployment, we would simply get higher and higher inflation.

It is striking to note that the changes in employment in this system are all by choice. Workers end idleness because they think, perhaps incorrectly, that real wages are higher. Workers voluntarily quit jobs when they discover that real wages are not as high as they wish.[7] Employers hire more workers when real costs decline. They let them go if workers insist on wages that drive costs too high. There are no workers who would be happy to take jobs at existing wages or even somewhat below them but cannot find them. There are no employers who would happily hire more workers at existing wages (seeing no problem in labor cost) but do not hire because they do not see how they can sell what they would produce.

This system does not usually recognize real-world difficulties that preclude price cutting to increase the sale of product, and wage cutting, directly stimulating the demand for labor, sufficient to put everybody to work. These difficulties may

---

[7] In terms of the usual definitions, these changes in employment may not even qualify as changes in *un*employment. To be counted as unemployed by the U.S. Bureau of Labor Statistics, a person has to be without a job *and looking for work*. A person not working because of the belief that real wages are generally too low may not currently be looking for work. There may thus be substantial fluctuations of employment in this system which are not fluctuations in *un*employment.

include employers that are reluctant to lower prices now—especially on durable goods like automobiles—because any increase in sales and production that might put more people to work would be at the expense of next year's market, in which they might be able to sell at higher prices and higher profits. They may include worker reluctance to accept jobs that would put them in long-term lower wage positions. They may include employer reluctance to cut wages lest their best workers take jobs elsewhere, leaving them with lower average wages but sufficiently lower average productivity to generate higher labor costs. And they may include the related problem that declines in wages and prices, rather than stimulating sales and employment, only generate the expectation that wages and prices will continue to fall. Employers may then hold off hiring while customers hold off buying.

THE DO-NOTHING—OR LITTLE—CONCLUSION

Ignoring all the forces that may generate substantial unemployment, which the market proves unable—or unable rapidly—to counteract, the conclusion of free marketeer Friedman was: don't try to stimulate the economy to reduce unemployment. Leave unemployment at whatever level the market determines. And that level would be what he called the "natural rate of unemployment," corresponding by this logic to the NAIRU, the nonaccelerating-inflation-rate of unemployment.

It hardly seems right to blame nature, or God, for unemployment, and, to be fair, Friedman did not do that. Rather, he argued that given worker preferences, the times people were out of work while changing jobs or looking for new ones, and given various imperfections in labor markets—Friedman would stress government interferences such as minimum wage laws—a certain amount of unemployment was inevitable. Keynes indeed had pointed up the "frictional" and "voluntary" unemployment, to which I referred above, and which need not be considered incompatible with what we would consider "full employment." Any efforts to get unemployment below the natural rate, as Friedman dubbed it, could have only temporary success, at the cost of higher inflation.

And that higher inflation would be permanent, unless unemployment increased above its natural rate. Only then would inflation decelerate. Hence the Friedman argument, and that of many fellow conservatives, that if indefinitely higher inflation is intolerable, there is no real possibility of lowering unemployment, at least by manipulating demand. There is only, at best, the choice of less unemployment now at the cost of more unemployment later.

If this reasoning is accepted, and I have to confess, to my dismay, that many economists came to accept it in the 1970s and 1980s,[8] the only remaining issue is just what that NAIRU or the natural rate of unemployment is. For those who don't go so far as to insist that the economy is always at its natural rate, when do we know that actual unemployment is too high so that we can do something to speed its return to the natural rate? Some, as suggested earlier, may think whatever *is* is natural, including unemployment rates as high as the 10.7 percent at the depth of the 1982–1983 recession. For the rest of the profession, however, there did seem to be compelling arguments, given the market imperfections that slowed adjustment, to move to reduce excessive unemployment.[9]

What then was the natural rate? My observation here again is that there was a political division. Conservatives argued that it was 6.5 percent, 7 percent, or even 7.5 percent. Liberals suggested it was 6 percent, with a few placing it perhaps at 5.5 or even 5 percent; my colleague, Robert Gordon, has it at 6.0 percent[10] and had it at that rate through all of the 1980s.

---

[8]Friedman presented his arguments in his presidential address to the American Economic Association, December 1967, and they proved very influential indeed.

[9]Even in the fall of 1991, however, with unemployment at 7 percent and rising to its recession peak, Charles Schultze, President Carter's chairman of the Council of Economic Advisers and another former president of the American Economic Association, was advising Dan Rostenkowski, the Democratic chairman of the House Ways and Means Committee, which was considering the desirability of trying to stimulate the economy, "Don't just do something; stand there!"

[10]*Macroeconomics,* 6th ed. (New York: HarperCollins, 1993), Appendix A.

The Congressional Budget Office estimates a somewhat more varying NAIRU, placed in 1992 at 5.6 percent. But congressional committees found few economists to testify in support of the Humphrey–Hawkins bill, which eventually became law, setting goals of 4 percent unemployment (although I do recall one hearing in which I was joined by now Nobel laureate Lawrence Klein of the University of Pennsylvania and Nancy Barrett, then of American University, in support of a Catholic Bishops' economic statement along those lines).

If these arguments hold, what is left? If the economy is generally at its natural rate of unemployment, larger budget deficits or other stimuli are only needed when unemployment, as in a significant recession, is clearly above its natural rate. For those who insist that the economy is somehow always at its natural rate, stimulus would never be indicated. But even those who are ready to advocate larger deficits to combat temporarily high unemployment may insist that over the long run the deficit should be kept down. In the long term, they argue, the economy oscillates about its natural rate.

Larger permanent deficits, by this argument, cannot increase average employment and output. At best they will only increase inflation. But since the Federal Reserve, the monetary authority, sympathetic to concerns of bankers and other losers from inflation, will then move to curb the money supply and raise interest rates, we will suffer the worst. We will have a reduction ("crowding out") of investment, thus sacrificing our long-run welfare. If we are not "spending our children's money," in Ross Perot's inaccurate phrase, we will be eating their seed corn.

THE INFAMOUS NAIRU

"Statistics," it has been said, "are the straightest line from an unreasonable assumption to a foregone conclusion." Some economic theory, I might suggest, also fits that quip. The theory and statistics used to construct and build policy on the basis of the NAIRU are prime examples.

Economists are always warning that the attractive easy solutions to problems may not work, that there is no free lunch, and that to get more of one thing we have to enjoy less of something else. Of course, frequently we are right. But one day, I hope not too far in the future, a historian of economic thought will record the whole concept of the NAIRU as one of the more bizarre and costly turns in the development of economic science.

For those anxious to attain high employment and economic growth, the NAIRU has been dismal indeed. It tells us that if we persist in trying to get and keep unemployment below it, we will have, not merely inflation, but accelerating inflation. Literally that might mean a very slowly accelerating inflation, like one-tenth of 1 percent per year. But somehow the term is used to imply that inflation will accelerate rapidly, conjuring up visions of Germans in the 1920s carrying marks in wheelbarrows and using money as wallpaper.

Taken literally, the concept suggests that we can always stop the acceleration by driving unemployment back to the NAIRU, but the argument is usually made that there are lags. Therefore, it may take time to raise unemployment enough (horrors!), and it may take more time before the higher unemployment stops the acceleration of inflation. Further, when the acceleration is finally stopped, inflation itself can be very high. It will then take excess unemployment—a rate of unemployment greater than the NAIRU—to drive inflation down again. With this scenario one may feel compelled to cry, as soldiers newly landed on foreign soil have been known to call out in sardonic humor to comrades about to join them, "Go back before it's too late." Don't try to reduce unemployment at all, lest you drive it inadvertently below the NAIRU and slip down a disastrous slope of inflation.

"RATIONAL EXPECTATIONS" AND ITS LIMITS

The NAIRU finds theoretical support in "rational expectations." This concept, initially applied to macroeconomics in the 1970s by Robert Lucas of the University of Chicago and Thomas Sargent, then at the University of Minnesota, essentially indicates that people or economic "agents" will not act stupidly.[11] They will take advantage of all available information and make decisions that maximize their own advantage. Applied to stock prices, the concept yielded the powerful hypothesis of efficient markets. One would not, for example, expect the market to generally be low Friday afternoons and high on Monday mornings. If it were, investors would notice and try to buy more on Fridays in order to sell on Mondays. Their very effort to do this would, however, raise prices on Fridays and lower them on Mondays, and thus eliminate the differential.

And indeed, to a considerable extent, the theory of efficient markets holds up, although there are many anomalies. These relate primarily to the fact that information is not costless and that the factors of risk and uncertainty may make optimizing behavior different from what it seems in a simple situation where agents choose between two certain and perfectly known prospects. It is irrational to buy item A for two dollars when item B is identical and available for one dollar. In that situation, our "representative" agent will always buy item B. Similarly, it would be irrational for a perfect market not to clear—for example, for an immediately perishable, one-of-a-kind commodity, for which there is some demand, to go unsold because sellers insisted on a higher price than buyers were willing to pay. Both sellers and buyers would be clear losers. The sellers would see their commodity go to waste without a sale and the buyers would not get something they wanted.

Alas, the world of economic decision making is not always, perhaps not often, that simple. It certainly is not for the unemployed worker or potential employer who, according to cer-

---

[11]See Robert E. Lucas, Jr., "Expectations and the Neutrality of Money," *Journal of Economic Theory,* vol. 4, April 1972, pp. 103–124; Lucas and Thomas P. Sargent, "After Keynesian Macroeconomics," Federal Reserve Bank of Minneapolis, *Quarterly Review,* vol. 3, Spring 1979, pp. 1–16; and Sargent and Neil Wallace, "Rational Expectations and the Theory of Economic Policy," *Journal of Monetary Economics,* vol. 2, April 1976, pp. 169–183.

tain pure theory, could eliminate unemployment if he or she would only agree to lower wages. There are uncertainties and heterogeneities and ignorance of opportunities and prospects that prevent employment from rising by these means.

Workers, as we suggested above, may worry that if they take lower pay now rather than hold out for a better future opportunity they will forever suffer lower wages. Employers may worry that workers who will accept lower wages are less able. All purchasers, including those of labor services, may hold off in the face of falling wages and prices in the expectation that they may yet fall further. And this still ignores the venerable fallacy of composition, the possibility that what is true for one worker or one firm or one market may not be true for all. If wages and prices were lower, demand in money terms might also be lower and the success of one unemployed worker in obtaining a job might be offset by the loss of one job by someone employed.

The pure foundations of the NAIRU, however, leave little room for such doubts. It sets aside the possibility that endemic problems of inadequate aggregate demand in the face of perpetually changing conditions generally prevent employment from being anywhere near full. Some advocates of the NAIRU explain unemployment in terms of voluntary decisions of workers to seek, hold, or relinquish employment. The late great British economist, Joan Robinson, an early youthful associate of Keynes, once wrote contemptuously of the idea that workers were always able to choose how much to work in terms of the neat calculus of equating the marginal disutility (extra pain) of work to the utility (benefit) of the real wage, as economic theory puts it. She suggested that rather than deciding whether the wage was worth accepting, workers faced the choice of accepting a job or starving.

It is obviously not that stark a choice in the modern welfare state, but that model of choice may be closer to reality than the one that has unemployment varying with workers' comparisons of actual and anticipated rates of inflation. As Franco Modigliani put it in his presidential address to the American Economic Association, the natural rate of unemployment hypothesis left the sharp downturns in employment associated with depressions and recessions to be viewed as the results of "epidemics of contagious laziness."

But in the NAIRU–natural rate model, again, people are working as much as they wish, given the information they have with regard to wages, prices, and inflation. Increasing demand for goods and services—through the fiscal stimulus of increased government spending or lower taxes or the monetary stimulus that might (temporarily) lower interest rates—could only increase employment temporarily by increasing inflation. Rational people sooner or later—and with experience it would tend to be sooner rather than later—adjust their expectations of inflation to the inflation that has occurred.[12] The attempt to maintain "too low" unemployment can only raise inflation further. In the simple formulation of the NAIRU, inflation each year—or month or week—equals previous inflation plus a fraction of the amount by which unemployment is below its acceleration point.[13] Unemployment be-

---

[12] Rational people make use of all available information in making their economic decisions. Continuing current inflation would certainly be information to utilize in forming expectations of inflation in the future. But should expected future inflation really adjust quickly and fully to actual inflation? The ultimate exemplar of rational expectations may be taken to be the person who does not stoop to pick up a $20 bill lying on the sidewalk. The reasoning behind not picking it up is that it must be known to be counterfeit; otherwise someone else would have picked it up already, since people are generally rational and no rational person would have left a real $20 bill lying on the sidewalk.

[13] Applying symbols, let $\dot{p}$ = inflation, let $\dot{p}^e$ = expected inflation, let u = actual unemployment, and let u^n = the "natural" rate of unemployment or the NAIRU. Now if $\dot{p}^e = \dot{p}_{-1}$, previous inflation or some weighted average of previous rates of inflation, we have:

$$\dot{p} = \dot{p}^e + \beta(u^n - u), \text{ or } \dot{p} - \dot{p}_{-1} = \beta(u^n - u),$$

where β is some positive number. Hence, if $u^n - u > 0$, that is, unemployment is below the NAIRU, $\dot{p} - \dot{p}_{-1} > 0$, or inflation has nowhere to go but up.

One crucial—and doubtful—assumption in all this is that $\dot{p}^e = \dot{p}_{-1}$, presumably based on the notion that "rational" agents shape their expectations of the future on the evidence they have and that the best evidence as to what inflation will be tomorrow is what it was yesterday. More generally, $\dot{p}^e = \alpha(\dot{p}_{-1})$, where $0 < \alpha < 1$. If rational people are not sure that higher than usual inflation will continue and make decisions on the possibility that it may go back to normal, the whole argument collapses. Unemployment can stay below its natural rate and inflation may not accelerate. And when unemployment goes down a bit, by this logic, inflation may well subside.

low the NAIRU then can only cause faster and faster inflation until, eventually, the authorities give up and allow (or encourage) really high unemployment to reverse the process.

IS THERE REALLY ANY KNOWN, RELEVANT FIXED NAIRU WE SHOULD NOT CROSS?

So economists and econometricians tried to find that magic point of acceleration. Clearly there is some rate, if only zero, below which unemployment cannot go. But this fact gives the NAIRU no more specific content than the famed—or infamous—Laffer napkin curve.[14] That was used to argue (to the incredulity of many) that because at very high tax rates—in fact at a rate of 100 percent—few or even none would choose to earn income and thus tax revenues would approach zero, *current* tax rates were such that lowering them would increase tax revenues.

As something of a practicing empirical econometrician, I have over the years often called for caution in letting our computers do the talking for us; in reality of course, they are our Charlie McCarthys, whose voices reflect the programming of their masters. At the least, devotees of the various estimates of the NAIRU might have warned that they could offer only uncertain probabilistic statements about possible future time paths of variables like unemployment and inflation. They could have said that a $50 billion fiscal stimulus package might, with varying probabilities, reduce unemployment by from 0.2 percent to 1.2 percent over the next year. This might in turn increase inflation from *minus* 0.5 percent to

---

[14] A spread-out, upside-down "U" on a graph with the rate of taxation on the horizontal axis and tax revenues on the vertical. At zero rates of taxation as well as at 100 percent rates there would be no tax revenues. Since in between these rates tax revenues were positive, there was a rate of taxation that would maximize tax revenues. Arthur Laffer, once at the University of Chicago, then in the Reagan administration, and since then the well-known head of his own consulting firm, suggested that we were at a rate of taxation beyond the peak of the curve and that lowering tax rates would actually increase tax revenues.

plus 1 percent over the next year; contrary to all the NAIRU reasoning it might actually reduce inflation as increased production spread capital and labor overhead and reduced a variety of average and marginal costs. And the further we got into the future, the more uncertain any of their probabilistic statements would be.

The NAIRU supporters might indeed have turned the whole analysis on its head. Instead of any given rate of inflation tending to perpetuate itself as inflation expectations adjust to actual inflation, any given rate of unemployment may tend to perpetuate itself unless something is done about it. This approach is the concept of "hysteresis," put forth in the past decade by distinguished economists Oliver Blanchard at MIT and Lawrence Summers, then at Harvard University,[15] and taken up by a number of others, including my Northwestern colleague, Robert Gordon. Much of Western Europe, after long having lower unemployment than the United States, has indeed found unemployment getting into and then seeming to perpetuate itself in double-digit rates, in spite of inflation rates exceeding ours.

Or those who would hang the economy on the NAIRU might have faced a few simple recent historical facts of American experience. For years we were told that efforts to reduce unemployment below a NAIRU of variously, 6.5 and 7 percent would either (1) do no good or (2) cause accelerating inflation. Then in 1988, 1989, and 1990, unemployment averaged successively 5.4 percent, 5.2 percent, and 5.4 percent. Probably the best overall measure of inflation, the change in the implicit price deflator for gross domestic product, went from 3.9 percent in 1988 to 4.4 percent in 1989 to 4.4 percent in 1990, and then to 3.9 percent in 1991. I eagerly await the econometric estimates of accelerating inflation that can come out of those figures.

---

[15]More recently vice president for economic research at the World Bank and currently assistant secretary for international economics in the U.S. Treasury Department. See Oliver J. Blanchard and Lawrence H. Summers, "Hysteresis and the European Unemployment Problem," in S. Fischer, ed., *NBER Macroeconomics Annual 1986*, pp. 15–17.

Were the 6.5 and 7.0 percent NAIRU estimates off the mark? Are there really inflationary dangers so great that we should eschew policies that might reduce unemployment again to the 5.0 percent rate it achieved briefly in March 1989 or the 5.1 percent rate it was at as recently as June 1990? What about the old 4 percent target of the Humphrey–Hawkins Act? Or better, the 3.4 percent average for 1969? Does it take a war to force unemployment down?

Over the past half-century, even excluding the earlier Great Depression of the 1930s, our official measures of actual unemployment have oscillated widely around measures of the "natural" rate, as may be noted in Figure 8.3. There is no credible evidence that these oscillations related to differences between actual and anticipated inflation or voluntary decisions of workers to seek more or less employment in response to changing perceptions of their real wage.

In Figure 8.4 we may be able to discern some evidence, though, if we do not want to be too exacting, that excesses of the "natural" rate over the actual rate have been associated with increases in inflation. This would seem to confirm the accelerationist view of the world. And more rigorous least-squares regressions would also seem to confirm this. Over the period 1950–1992 (excluding the immediate postwar years of rapid deceleration of inflation), each percentage point of the difference between the NAIRU and actual unemployment was associated on the average with 0.41 percentage points per annum of increase in inflation, and this result was statistically significant.[16]

If we confine our analysis to the 1970–1992 period, we would seem to have even more evidence of acceleration. Each percentage point the NAIRU exceeded actual unemployment was associated with a 0.78 percentage point *increase* in inflation, and each percentage point of excess unemployment with a 0.78 percentage point *decrease* in inflation. For this period, though, the constant term in the regression was 0.62, im-

---

[16]Standard error of .12 (t = 3.46) in an AR(1) regression.

Figure 8.3 *Actual and "Natural" Unemployment*
in the United States, 1947–1992

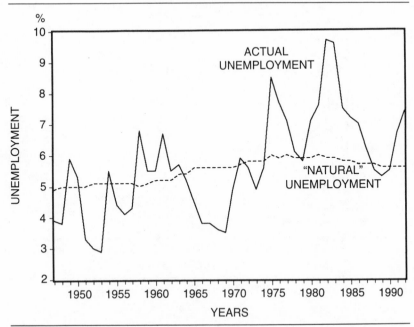

Sources: Congressional Budget Office, *The Economic and Budget Outlook: Fiscal Years 1994–1998,* January 1993, Table E-1, p. 123; Robert J. Gordon, *Macroeconomics,* 6th ed. (New York: HarperCollins) 1993, Table A-1, p. A2; and *Economic Report of the President,* 1993, Table B-30, p. 382.

plying that unemployment equal to the natural rate would generate not constant inflation but an inflation accelerating at 0.62 percentage points per year.[17]

There remains one critical issue to be resolved: Is the relation symmetrical? Section A of Table 8.1 reveals that years in which unemployment was above the NAIRU were years in which inflation, on the average, slowed, while years when unemployment was below the NAIRU were years when it

---

[17] It may be argued that this last result is a consequence of "supply shocks." Much of the inflation of the 1970s and early 1980s, it should have been clear, came from the huge increases in petroleum prices and energy prices in general imposed on the world by OPEC. This had little or nothing to do with the state of employment or unemployment in the United States, or anywhere else.

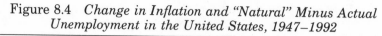

Figure 8.4   *Change in Inflation and "Natural" Minus Actual*
Unemployment in the United States, 1947–1992

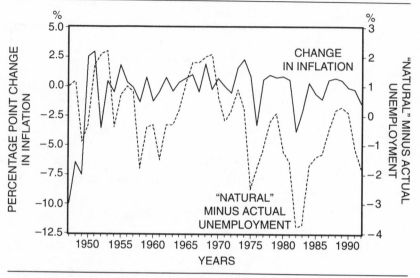

Sources: Data used in Table 8.1 and Figures 8.2A, 8.2B, and 8.3.

accelerated. The differences were not, however, statistically significant.[18] Is it possible, though, that as unemployment rises above the NAIRU it has a much more substantial and significant effect of driving down inflation than declines of unemployment below the NAIRU have in raising inflation?

Regressions separating out the two cases, reported in Section B of Table 8.1, seem to confirm this possibility. Over the entire 1950–1992 period, each percentage point that unemployment rose above the natural rate was associated with a 0.85 percentage point decrease in inflation, and this figure

---

[18] In years that unemployment was above the NAIRU, inflation decreased by 0.34 percentage points on the average over the entire 1950–1992 period, and 0.53 percentage points over the years 1970–1992. Inflation increased in years that unemployment was below the NAIRU, 0.55 percentage points on the average over the entire period and 0.73 percentage points over the 1970–1992 period. The highest t-statistic in connection with these numbers, for the low unemployment figure over the whole period, was 1.75, with a 2-tail significance level of 0.08.

Table 8.1 *Change in Inflation and Actual Minus "Natural"*
Unemployment (NAIRU), 1950–1992

A. Average percentage point change in inflation for years in
which unemployment is greater than NAIRU and years in which
unemployment is less than NAIRU

	1950–1992	1970–1992	1980–1992
All Observations	0.07	−0.09	−0.46
Unemployment greater than NAIRU	−0.34	−0.53	−0.71
Unemployment less than NAIRU	0.55	0.74	0.38

B. Percentage point change in inflation per percentage point difference between unemployment and NAIRU

	1950–1992	1970–1992	1980–1992
All Observations	−0.41	−0.78	−0.86
Unemployment greater than NAIRU	−0.85	−0.84	−1.04
Unemployment less than NAIRU	−0.24	0.27	−2.70

Source: Prepared by author from data used in Figures 8.2A, 8.2B, and 8.3.

was statistically significant.[19] But each percentage point that
unemployment fell *below* the natural rate was also associated
with a greater decrease in inflation, in this case (a nonsignificant) 0.24 percentage points. For the later period, 1970–1992,
more unemployment above the NAIRU did again seem to
drive down inflation—0.84 percentage points more reduction
of inflation for each percentage point of excess unemployment,
and the figure was again statistically significant.[20] Unemployment further below the NAIRU did over this period seem
to be associated with a somewhat greater increase in inflation, but the coefficient was only a quite nonsignificant 0.27;[21]

[19] Standard error of 0.18 (t = −4.63) in an AR(1) regression.
[20] Standard error of 0.22 (t = −3.77) in an AR(1) regression.
[21] The lack of statistical significance may be attributed to the fact that there was
little variance in the observations of employment below the NAIRU. Over the 1950–

each additional percentage point that unemployment fell below the NAIRU was associated with a 0.27 percentage point acceleration of inflation.

If we restrict our statistics to the most recent period, from 1980 to 1992, we again find more unemployment above the NAIRU associated with substantial and significant reductions in inflation, 1.043 percentage points reduction in inflation per 1 percentage point of additional unemployment[22]— the declines in inflation with the severe 1982–1983 recession (and the concurrent drop in petroleum prices) undoubtedly contributing to this relation. The few years that unemployment was below the NAIRU could be projected to associate each additional percentage point less of unemployment with a 2.70 percentage point *decrease* in inflation, but this result was not at all significant.[23]

In some periods of high employment, particularly those associated with wars, there has been some tendency for prices to rise more. But one would need a vivid imagination—or a very imaginatively programmed computer—to draw the conclusion that sustained high employment created significantly accelerating, let alone permanently accelerating, inflation. And now, finally, in the past few years, there have been rigorous challenges by mathematical economic theorists to the notion that there is any unique, determinate, and stable natural rate of unemployment.[24]

1992 period it was never more than 2.2 percentage points below the NAIRU and during the years 1970–1992 never more than 0.9 percentage points below. But given the lack of direct statistical evidence (because unemployment rarely dipped much below the NAIRU), it is hard to feel confident about projections that indicate that if it *did*, we would have significant accelerating inflation.

[22] Standard error of 0.26 (t-statistic of −4.07).

[23] Standard error of 3.22.

[24] See Dale T. Mortensen, "The Persistence and Indeterminacy of Unemployment in Search Equilibrium," *Scandinavian Journal of Economics,* vol. 91, no. 2 (1989), pp. 347–370 and "Which 'Natural' Rate?, The Role of Bulls, Bears and Other Animal Spirits," Northwestern University, September 1993; Russell W. Cooper and John Andrews, "Coordinating Coordination Failures in Keynesian Models," *Quarterly Journal of Economics,* vol. 103 (August 1988), pp. 441–463; and Peter Howitt and R. Preston McAfee, "Stability of Equilibria with Externalities," *Quarterly Journal of Economics,* vol. 103 (May 1988), pp. 261–277, and "Animal Spirits," *American*

OR SHOULD WE COMBAT UNEMPLOYMENT WITHOUT HINDRANCE FROM A BUGABOO OF INFLATION?

Can I guarantee that measures—short of war—to reduce unemployment to 3.4 percent will not increase the rate of inflation? No! Can anyone be sure it *will* increase inflation, let alone by how much or that the inflation will continue accelerating? I daresay no. As a case in point, consider Japan, whose political leaders in the summer of 1993 proposed a major stimulus package—much larger than the Clinton package blocked by solid Republican opposition—in the face of unemployment still under 3 percent and inflation next to zero.

And I can suggest further that many measures of stimulus—both short-term and long-term—can involve government subsidies and investment that will lower labor and business costs and thus tend to lower prices and inflation. These could include job training and subsidies to hire the unemployed and comprehensive apprentice programs that would tie secondary education, for those not going further, to jobs. They could involve shifting taxation from sales and excise and payroll taxes that tend to raise costs and prices to taxes

---

Economic Review, vol. 82 (June 1992), pp. 493–507. How then can we explain the long ascendancy of natural rate and NAIRU doctrine? How explain the associated misapplication of rational expectations, and the assumption that those unemployed were all without jobs by choice, to justify inaction in the face of chronic and varying excess unemployment? We may ponder the observations of Keynes on the victory, long before, of Ricardian doctrine, which also ruled out correctable insufficiencies in aggregate demand as sources of unemployment.

The completeness of the Ricardian victory is something of a curiosity and a mystery. . . . That it reached conclusions quite different from what the ordinary uninstructed person would expect, added, I suppose to its intellectual prestige. That its teaching, translated into practice, was austere and often unpalatable, lent it virtue. That it was adapted to carry a vast and consistent logical superstructure, gave it beauty. That it could explain much social injustice and apparent cruelty as an inevitable incident in the scheme of progress, and the attempt to change such things as likely on the whole to do more harm than good, commended it to authority. That it afforded a measure of justification to the free activities of the individual capitalist, attracted to it the support of the dominant social force behind authority.—John Maynard Keynes, *The General Theory of Employment, Interest and Money,* pp. 32–33.

on all income and capital gains, if not wealth, that would hold down excessive nominal demand and thus lower prices.

And if we are really concerned about inflation, we might tackle all the more aggressively the interferences with free-market forces—many imposed by government at the behest of particular interest groups—which tend to keep prices from falling in response to competition at home or from abroad. Just for starters, we could remove all tariffs and import quotas, whether imposed directly by us or by others on their exports to the United States; Japanese automobile manufacturers have laughed all the way to the bank as the restrictions on Japanese cars available in the United States prevented increases in supply to meet high demand and enabled their manufacturers to keep prices high and reap huge profits. We could also eliminate the requirements that goods be transported in American ships at rates more than twice world shipping charges. We could end the practice of keeping up the prices of highly productive American agriculture.

In any event, to adapt the phrase of William Jennings Bryan of a century ago, we must not crucify our country and its economy on the cross of misguided and misaddressed fears of inflation. Neither the fiscal stimulus of structural budget deficits nor monetary stimulus directed at reducing unemployment in the United States has yet caused permanently accelerating inflation, or much inflation at all. Most of the inflation of the postwar period has come instead from supply shocks—chiefly the great run-up of petroleum prices in the 1970s and early 1980s.

Neither God nor nature decreed that involuntary unemployment need always be with us, nor that there is a rate of unemployment below what is "natural" but not below what is really full, which necessarily entails accelerating inflation. Once we accept that, it makes all the difference in what we can do to get our economy on the right, fast track.

CHAPTER 9

What's to Be Done?

"We're broke! Before we can do anything we have to get our finances together."—Daniel Patrick Moynihan, chairman of the Senate Finance Committee, on NBC News, April 11, 1993.

"The national debt is no doubt a terrible thing. One day it will ruin us all. Everybody says it, so it must be true. But it is 300 years old and it hasn't ruined us yet. On the contrary, sinking deeper into debt, first Britain and then the United States created the richest, freest, and most dynamic societies the world has ever known. These two feckless debtors beat back tyrants like Napoleon and Hitler. They settled continents, created new technologies, and flew to the moon."—Walter Russell Mead, *Los Angeles Times*, January 17, 1993.

"Now there are a bloc of people in the Senate, including some Democrats, who believe that the only thing that matters is to reduce the deficit . . . , but I just disagree with them. I don't think that's the only thing that matters; I believe that investing in the future matters, too. And I believe that if we don't change the spending patterns of the Government, and invest and put some of the American people back to work and create some—millions—of jobs, that we're not going to have an economic recovery."—Bill Clinton, press conference, as reported in the *New York Times*, March 24, 1993.

What does matter? What counts? Taxes, spending, money, prices—these are all means to an end. The end, I have

195

pointed out, is economic welfare now and in the future. We can begin to measure it by gross domestic product or gross national product and, as a contribution to the future, national saving. But our GDP or GNP may have to be adjusted for the excluded nonmarket outputs and the misclassification of product (that is, final versus intermediate). Most important, measurement of the national saving must be comprehensive, including all investment, public and private, tangible and intangible or human, as well as gains, or losses, of wealth in connection with changing market values of foreign investments.

TAXES, SPENDING, AND DEMAND

Taxes serve a number of purposes. The most important is to reduce the purchasing power of taxpayers. Resources are then freed from production of the goods and services that they would otherwise buy. It is in this sense, in real terms, that taxes pay for government expenditures.

For example, suppose the FBI needs some new cars. An increase in personal income taxes—or better, gasoline taxes—may discourage individuals from buying new automobiles. GM, Chrysler, or Ford can then sell the government cars that would otherwise be bought by private consumers.

Less individual consumption means less production of consumer goods or services. Now suppose that government holds the lid on spending and does not utilize the resources freed from consumer goods production, even as it increases taxes. According to classical analysis, that not only leaves resources available for the production of capital goods—of new machinery, factories, office buildings, shopping centers, and houses—but also brings about their utilization for that purpose. But whether this occurs is doubtful. At most, we can say, "It depends."

It depends on whether the possible purchasers of capital goods feel it is profitable to make those purchases. If the economy is slumping and/or there is already a surfeit of capital goods, they will not make the purchases. If interest rates, borrowing costs, or, more generally, the cost of capital is high, the purchases will not be made. In these cases, the reduction in consumption as a result of increased taxes will cause less private investment, as history has shown. Increases in taxes, unmatched by increases in government spending, have generally meant both less consumption and less investment. That means less employment and less output, now and in the future.

Conservatives are quick to agree. "No new taxes!" they proclaim.[1] While seeing little justification for increasing taxes in the size of the deficit, conservatives urge that I recognize the real problem—too much government spending. Raising taxes is bad but cutting spending is good, they insist. But are increases in taxes and cuts in spending all that different?

President Clinton has said,[2] "All spending is not the same, whether it's in the public or the private sector ... [T]here really is a fundamental difference between investment and consumption." What public spending does is vitally important from the standpoint of productivity and long-run growth. But more government spending in the slack economy that we often have, like lower taxes (both of which increase deficits), is good from the standpoint of demand and purchasing power and moving us toward full employment and full utilization of our existing capacity. Cuts in government spending hurt.

The periodic furor over elimination of military bases is illustrative. This entails cuts in government spending. Clos-

---

[1] Recent letters to the *Harvard Business Review,* in response to an article I published there, suggest considerable conservative support, as well, of my thesis that federal budget deficits are hopelessly mismeasured and that, contrary to conventional wisdom, they are not in themselves a critical problem. Paul Craig Roberts, conservative writer for the *Washington Times* and *Business Week,* and a former Reagan administration Treasury official, "admires" me and my views on the deficit. Edwin Rubenstein, economic analyst for William Buckley's *National Review,* wishes Washington would listen to me. Allan Meltzer, of Carnegie-Mellon and the American Enterprise Institute and head of the Shadow Open Market Committee, says I "perform an important public service."

[2] At Little Rock in his December 1992 economic conference, in introducing me as "sort of the country's foremost advocate that we have overstated our real debt because we don't take account of capital investments and growth."

ings proposed in 1993 were estimated to reduce outlays by some $5 billion per year. But their immediate effect is to destroy jobs, not only of service personnel, but of those in the affected communities—and indeed, around the nation. Closings of the navy base and shipyards in Charleston, South Carolina, will directly cost 20,000 jobs, closings in California, 25,000 jobs. Like stuck pigs, senators and congressmen in the affected states and districts, whatever their attitude on the overall defense program, squeal in protest.

Are other spending cuts fundamentally different? Any reduction in government spending for goods and services means a reduction in the production of these goods and services and loss of employment for those engaged in that production. This is true, whether it is for pothole repair, post office construction, or paperwork in government offices.

Reductions in government outlays that are not for the purchase of goods and services have similar, if more indirect, effects. If people on social security are denied cost-of-living allowances, they spend less for goods and services—for movies, for clothes, for restaurants, for travel, perhaps less even for food or pharmaceuticals. Businesses that sell these goods and services lose income and need fewer workers.

The essential similarity of tax increases and spending cuts is driven home by the semantic battle about increased taxation of social security benefits. The Clinton administration, like the Reagan administration, chooses to classify it as a spending reduction—which is attractive to the public at large—ostensibly because it entails reductions in net outlays for social security.[3] Critics insist that it is really exactly what it appears to be—a tax increase. But does it make any economic difference? Suppose social security benefit payments were reduced at the source by an amount corresponding to what would otherwise be taken away in taxes, probably by

---

[3] Social security retirement benefits had, until the 1980s, always been free of taxation. During the Reagan administration net social security payments were reduced by including in taxable income 50 percent of benefits of recipients with substantial total incomes. The Clinton administration, as pointed out in Chapter 8, has brought about an increase of this figure to 85 percent.

withholding, so that the checks would be the same. Would the amount spent by retirees be different?

The results are the same for any other reductions in government spending or outlays, including those for interest payments on the government debt. Almost everybody bemoans the interest burden. But that "burden" of $180 billion on the Treasury constitutes interest payments to the American households and banks and businesses that own the Treasury's debt (as well as to social security and other government trust funds). If we could wave a magic wand and wipe out Treasury interest payments, we would have a lot of desperate people who had lost the income from savings bonds, Treasury bills, notes, and bonds, and the pension funds that were holding them. This in turn would mean less spending on goods and services, less production, and less employment for a lot of other people.

THE SUPPLY-SIDE—LABOR AND CAPITAL AND SAVING

I should, however, qualify these statements. Taxes and spending affect not only demand, but also supply, as so-called supply-siders keep reminding us. More generally, they affect behavior. Taxes on labor income are supposed to discourage work. Taxes on capital income are supposed to discourage capital investment and saving. Sin taxes on liquor and tobacco, it is hoped, may discourage their production as well as drinking and smoking. Taxes on energy will raise its cost and reduce both the quantity demanded and the quantity supplied.

In general, taxes on factors of production—labor, land, and natural resources, or capital—will raise their costs. Such taxes, as well as direct taxes on output, will raise the prices of goods and services. They will thus negate efforts to combat inflation. They may also make efforts to attain high employment more difficult to the extent that the monetary authority deems it necessary to curb aggregate demand in order to combat the increases in prices brought on by reductions in supply or increases in costs. If maximum employment and aggregate output are prime objectives, as they should be, the monetary authority should be stimulative in the face of taxes reducing supply or raising costs. This may result in still higher prices but less reduction in total output and employment.[4]

Government spending for unemployment benefits may induce employers to lay off workers rather than keep them on at reduced hours—which would leave them without unemployment pay—when business is slack. It may also reduce the pressure on workers to keep jobs or to find new ones quickly. Government social security spending may cause earlier retirement. Government farm subsidies may maintain resources in unneeded agricultural pursuits and keep farmers and farm labor from moving into other work more useful to the economy.

These considerations suggest that raising taxes has costs and cutting government spending has benefits that should be taken into account. But they may not be as decisive as some would have us believe. Income taxes, an important example, are supposed to discourage labor and encourage leisure. The cost of an extra hour of leisure—an hour less of work—may be viewed as a loss of earnings. But the relevant earnings are earnings after taxes. Higher marginal income tax rates reduce the after-tax earnings from the last hours worked or from additional hours of labor that might be contemplated. They hence lower the cost, in foregone wages, of enjoying more leisure; the higher marginal income tax rates induce us to "buy" more leisure, that is, reduce our work hours.

---

[4] A special WEFA model report in June 1993 suggested that replacement of the energy tax in the Clinton economic program with comparable reductions in nondefense government spending for goods and services would result in a smaller reduction in GDP. This undoubtedly reflected the assumption in the model that the monetary authority would not have accommodated the higher prices that would have been generated by the energy tax. It should come as no surprise that resultant reductions in the real supply of money would add to the reductions in aggregate demand for goods and services brought on by the loss in real purchasing power as a result of the tax.

One could raise taxes, however, by eliminating various loopholes rather than increasing the marginal rates. It is these rates at the margin, on each *additional* dollar of income, that have a direct effect on a decision whether to work an extra hour or take a job or not. Most economists are wisely agreed on the virtue of minimizing the exemptions, deductions, credits, and incentives so that any given amount of tax revenues can be raised with the lowest possible tax *rates*.

It may further be argued, in the technical terms of economists, that we must recognize both substitution and income effects. A higher tax rate may well discourage the activity being taxed by inducing us to substitute another activity that is not taxed—for example, leisure (or untaxed nonmarket labor) for market labor. But a higher tax rate also leaves us with less after-tax income. It may therefore induce us to work harder to make up for the lost income. Which effect dominates, the substitution effect (which in this instance would make us work less) or the income effect (which would make us work more) cannot be determined a priori.

Increases in taxes achieved by increasing the tax base and not raising marginal rates would have only an income effect. Since the tax increases would leave us poorer, we would be inclined to work more to make up the lost after-tax income.

Similar arguments apply to saving. Does taxation of capital income—the income from accumulated savings—discourage saving? That depends on the relative strength of the substitution and income effects.

The issue is well illustrated in terms of how much we save to finance our retirement. We might calculate for example— or pension fund managers could calculate for us—that, with a 6 percent return, the savings we set aside each month plus the earnings on those savings until we begin to withdraw retirement dollars will finance the retirement to which we aspire. But suppose a one-third tax is imposed on the return on savings, reducing the net return to 4 percent. What is accumulated each year on previous savings is less.

On the one hand, this generates a substitution effect

against saving. Achieving any given amount of retirement benefits now requires more current saving. We may decide it is not worth it. Since retirement has become more expensive in terms of what we have to give up now in saving, we may decide to save less, and substitute more current consumption.

On the other hand, since our lifetime income is reduced by the tax on our earnings from accumulated savings, there is an income effect; our lower expected incomes induce us to reduce our consumption now, thus increasing current saving. And by increasing what we set aside each month, we will prevent our retirement benefits from taking all of the hit from the tax on earnings from savings. If this income effect dominates the substitution effect, the tax reducing the return on savings will thus cause more saving rather than less.

One might think that over the long run, as in saving for retirement, the income effect is likely to prove more important. Relatively small differences in rates of return, if accumulated over many years, will make large differences in the income and wealth of those who are in the position to save in their early years. People wishing to retire with an annual pension equal to, say, 80 percent of their annual wages while working will find the necessary amount considerably greater if the annual rate of real return on those accumulated savings is only 4 percent. This suggests that higher taxes on investment income would actually cause *more* saving.

Whether the income or substitution effect dominates is, however, an empirical question, which may well merit more study. What should be clear, though, is that there is little basis for confidence in the oft-repeated statement that higher income taxes, except to the extent they slow the economy, discourage saving.

Again, if we increased the base for taxation by eliminating or reducing exemptions and deductions, without raising marginal rates, we would have only an income effect. We would thus clearly be motivated to save more—at least of assets whose returns are not newly included in the tax base—to accumulate our desired retirement funds.

HIGH TAX RATES ON THE POOR

There are instances where the marginal effective tax rate is so high that the substitution effect clearly dominates and discourages labor. These are not, however, at the high end of the income scale, where supply-siders, at least some of the conservatives among them, seem most often to focus. We might ask what change in behavior to expect from corporate executives faced with an increase in their marginal tax rate from 31 percent to 36 percent or even, with a surtax, to 39.6 percent. I doubt many will decide not to work as hard and risk getting off the corporate success ladder.

Where the high marginal rates turn out to be clearly overwhelming is at the lower end of the income scale, for those on welfare, and for middle-income taxpayers on social security (see Chapter 6). In the case of women on AFDC, additional income (beyond a small minimum) results in a loss of welfare payments. There may also be a loss of food stamps, low-rent housing subsidies, and medicaid benefits. Finally, social security taxes and possibly even income taxes have to be paid on the additional earnings. Welfare recipients contemplating the relatively low-wage jobs that may be available to them may face a combination of loss of benefits and tax increases that is more than the additional income they would get from working. They would be worse off with a job than staying on welfare. Small wonder that there are successive generations living in such dependency and the welfare rolls swell!

But let us return to the problem of demand, to the loss in employment and output *and* in saving and investment that I have indicated might occur as a result of either tax increases or cuts in government spending. There may be qualifications or complications here as well. If somehow aggregate demand is very brisk, the lost consumption demand may be quickly replaced by other consumption or, if business sees profitable investment opportunities, by the production of capital goods. These are big ifs, but they cannot be ignored. We shall have to consider when they may become relevant on their own, or what we can do to make them relevant.

MONEY ISN'T EVERYTHING

That brings us back to the role of money. If people had more money, regardless of the taxes they pay or the benefits they receive from government outlays, would they spend more? If they had more money, might they "invest" more?

To begin, we have to distinguish carefully between money and wealth. Wealth can take many forms—tangible goods, stocks and bonds, as well as money. If the Treasury were to print a billion hundred-dollar bills and drop them from planes to where they would all be picked up, the public would be $100 billion richer, that is, with $100 billion more of wealth. Then we would surely spend more.

A similar result would be achieved if the government were to call in all of the unemployed—or anybody else—and give them $100 billion dollars, or if it were to print $100 billion and use it to pay people to repair potholes, build new post offices, or sit at desks in government offices. Increases in the quantity of money, which constitute increases in the wealth of the public, will generate more spending.

But these increases in the quantity of money are brought about by what is classified as "deficit spending"—financed in this case by the creation of money instead of borrowing. They hardly qualify as antidotes to reductions of deficit spending. They *are* deficit spending. In an accounting sense they may be thought of as adding to the noninterest-bearing debt of the government instead of the interest-bearing debt. In a very real economic sense, they correspondingly add to the non-interest-bearing assets of the public instead of their interest-bearing assets.

The way money is normally created in our economy, aside from deficit spending, is quite different, as I pointed out in Chapter 7. It involves an exchange of debt, with a generally trivial change in wealth. Where it originates, when it is undertaken as a government policy measure, is usually in the Federal Reserve's purchase of Treasury securities in the open market. Sellers of these securities receive checks drawn on Federal Reserve banks. As they deposit these checks, their holdings of money, in the form of bank deposits, increase. But their holdings of Treasury securities are reduced by a like amount.[5] There is therefore no wealth effect, as in the case of plane drops of hundred-dollar bills or deficit spending financed by money creation.

This does not mean that increases in the quantity of money brought on by Federal Reserve open-market purchases have no effect. But their effects are much less direct and, as I have noted, considerably more doubtful.

First, it should be realized that a major hoped-for effect of Federal Reserve open-market purchases is increased liquidity by banks (and other depository institutions). Those who sell Treasury securities to the Fed put the proceeds of their sales—Federal Reserve checks or wire transfers or whatever—in banks and hence give them reserves, in the form of additional Federal Reserve balances. Given fractional reserve requirements, chiefly against checkable deposits, the increased reserves are expected to make it possible for banks to make additional loans, which may directly finance investment, and further increase the quantity of money. Again this increase in the quantity of money in itself does not add to wealth; the public has more money but it also has more debt to banks. The new houses or business plant and equipment that the loans may finance do, however, constitute additional wealth, and this and the income generated in their production will lead to more consumption and saving.

Banks' loans and broader, more relevant, measures of money—as I have pointed out—relate to more than checkable bank deposits subject to Fed Reserve requirements. Yet it is only these that are directly affected by the Federal Reserve

---

[5]Except to the extent the Federal Reserve purchases drove up the price of these securities so that their sellers—as well as those still holding such securities—find their wealth somewhat more than before the Fed entered the market.

balances—part of the monetary base—that the Federal Reserve may control reasonably well, if it chooses. The open-market operations of the Fed to increase bank reserves turn out therefore to have a tenuous relation with the total quantity of money and credit. The Fed is frequently criticized for failing to meet its money growth targets; the money supply strays repeatedly out of its indicated range. That would appear, however, to be what is to be expected, given the nature of our banking system and the role of the Federal Reserve.

A further problem relates to just how much effect changes in the quantity of reserves and money will have on interest rates and other means of rationing credit. Clearly they can have a big effect on short-term rates. In the summer of 1993, riskless Treasury bills offered returns of less than 3 percent, as against 14 percent a dozen years earlier. The high rates in 1981 related in part, however, to much higher expected rates of inflation. The interest rates on the long-term corporate bonds relevant to business investment fell much less, from some 14 percent to 8 percent on high-grade securities. Given the lower marginal rates applicable to tax-deductible business interest costs and the lower rates of inflation and expected inflation, the *real,* after-tax long-term interest rate was little, if at all, lower than in 1981. Indeed, with reasonable assumptions about inflation expectations, real long-term, after-tax interest costs to business are probably higher now than a dozen years ago.[6]

The relative imperviousness of long-term rates to downward pressure is readily explained in economic theory and

---

[6]With inflation as measured by the GNP implicit price deflator running over 10 percent in 1980, expected annual inflation over the years ahead may well have risen to, say, 8 percent. It is hardly reasonable for anticipated inflation rates today to be more than the current 3 percent. That would mean that corresponding to rates of decline in nominal rates from 14 percent to 8 percent would be a decline of only 1 percentage point, from 6 percent to 5 percent in real rates. But now, taking into account taxes, the comparison is all the more dramatic. With marginal tax rates on business income then averaging perhaps 40 percent and now 33 percent, we find that the real *after-tax* rates have moved from (14 percent × .6) minus 8 percent, or 0.4 percent, to (8 percent × 2/3) minus 3 percent, or 2⅓ percent. Real interest rates would have risen some two percentage points!

had indeed an important role in Keynesian economics. Long-term rates will, after all, approximate an average of expected future short-term rates; if they were different, investors could arbitrage, borrowing short to lend long or vice versa. And when current short-term rates are low, the anticipation, or merely the risk, that they will get higher in the future means an aversion to lending long unless lenders are rewarded with a premium in the form of higher long-term rates.

Many economists—and I certainly agree with them—believe the Fed should try harder to bring long-term rates down by convincing investors through their deeds as well as words that they will keep short-term rates low in the future. But the Fed generally fails to do this, and that limits all the more its ability to lower long-term rates. Long-term rates are essentially an average of expected short-term rates, adjusted for risk of change in market value of securities in the interval. Action to lower short-term rates now can only lower long-term rates significantly to the extent that investors are convinced that short-term rates will be lower over that long-term future.[7] And there is an ultimate limit to any possible low-

---

[7] Assume the one-year rate of interest is 3 percent but that the rate of interest on one-year securities is expected to be 7 percent next year. The rate of interest on two-year securities, now, would then hardly differ from 5 percent, the amount that investors would expect to average by lending at 3 percent for one year and then taking the proceeds and lending again for one year at 7 percent. If the rate of interest on the two-year securities were less than 5 percent, they would not be bought until their cost fell to such a point that the return was 5 percent. And if the rate on these securities were above 5 percent, investors would rush to buy them, raising their cost so that the return was lowered to 5 percent.

Those looking for lower interest rates to stimulate the economy can only be dismayed by the posture taken by the Federal Reserve in July 1993. As reported by Rick Wartzman in *The Wall Street Journal*, July 23, 1993:

Federal Reserve Chairman Alan Greenspan said today that although he doesn't see any major threat of inflation now, the central bank will undoubtedly be forced to raise interest rates sometime down the road.

"The signal we are endeavoring to send here is that at some point, rates are going to have to move up," Mr. Greenspan told the Senate Banking Committee. . . .

Mr. Greenspan stressed that "we don't know where or when such changes" in interest rates would take place. But he said it was inevitable that rates would need to be raised as consumers and businesses pay off the debt they accumulated in the 1980s and the economy begins to expand more rapidly. Brisker eco-

ering of long-term rates, since we know that all rates, long and short, must remain positive. Nobody will lend money if the borrower will pay back to the lender less than what was lent.

THE RESPONSE OF PRIVATE INVESTMENT

If the fall of long-term interest rates is limited, there may have to be a substantial response of investment to what falls in interest rates do occur. The critical and crucial judgment of Keynes, and one in which most business executives would concur, is that the rate of interest, while not without significance, is not of overwhelming importance to investment decisions. If the expected profitability of new investment is high, it will be undertaken in the face of high interest costs. If the expected profitability is low—and certainly if it is nil— the investment will not be undertaken, regardless of the interest rate.

What then determines the expected profitability of investment? Critical is the need for additional plant and equipment, which occurs when current and expected future demand indicate a need for capacity beyond what is currently available. Upward of half of all business investment is undertaken in response to the need to increase production. A few illustrative numbers can make clear the dependence of investment demand on the growth in output.

Understand first that investment is the addition to existing capital. Bureau of Economic Analysis estimates indicate that the current cost (or replacement cost) measure of the gross stock of fixed private capital is about 3.5 times the net domestic product produced by business; roughly $18.2 trillion of plant and equipment are used to produce about $5.2 trillion of output. To maintain this ratio, capital has to be increased

---

nomic growth "doesn't necessarily engender inflationary pressures," Mr. Greenspan said, "but we have to be vigilant to make certain" that prices remain under control.

at the same rate as output. Assume a 3-percent per year growth in output. This would generate a need for a 3 percent increase in capital to maintain the same ratio. Given the existing stock of $18.2 trillion, that comes to $546 billion of net investment. With total fixed investment at about $800 billion, that would mean 68 percent of investment is generated by the need to keep up with growth in the economy. (The other 32 percent is replacement of existing stock as it wears out or becomes obsolete.) It is instructive to note that under these simple assumptions—which may not, however, be irrelevant to the real economy—a fall in the rate of growth of only one percentage point, from 3 percent to 2 percent, would reduce the demand for capacity-increasing investment by no less than $182 billion. This would mean a decline of some 22 percent in gross private domestic investment in fixed capital.[8]

All this is to say that the moderate changes in real long-term interest rates that occur cannot be expected to generate high investment if the economy is in a slump. And that brings us back to the central issue. Assume we have major cuts in government expenditures and increases in taxes, no matter what the mixture of the two. The associated reductions in the structural deficit may be expected to reduce aggregate demand—the amounts that households, business, and government together are ready to purchase. That can only reduce output, income, and employment, and with them, saving and investment, unless a countervailing force develops. The logic of those who support such a program—and the rationale accepted by the Clinton administration—is that this countervailing force will be lower long-term interest rates. These would be generated by the market expectations that future government borrowing will be less and the encouragement given by a cooperating Federal Reserve. It was not without significance that Alan Greenspan sat between Hillary Clinton

---

[8]This result is in line with the classical "acceleration principle," going back to the French economist, A. Aftalion, and in its first major American rendition, J.M. Clark. It indicates that the rate of investment demand depends, in part, upon the acceleration of the rate of aggregate demand or output.

and Tipper Gore as President Clinton delivered his State of the Union economic message in February 1993.

Will it work? One cannot dogmatically assert that it will, or that it will not. It depends. If the economy remains sluggish, with little upward lift, it is most likely that the fiscal restraint will overwhelm the expansionary effect of lower interest rates. The economy will slump and saving and investment will be depressed.

If the economy is moving into a brisk upturn, a stimulatory monetary policy may prove sufficient to keep it moving up, despite the loss of purchasing power stemming from the reduction in the structural deficit. If the addition of more productive capacity is indicated by the growth of the economy, the availability of relatively lower-cost financing may tip the scales in favor of investing now rather than waiting to make sure the growth in product demand is sustained. This brings into focus the Clinton administration's recommendations of a short-term stimulus of increased government spending, chiefly on infrastructure, and temporary tax incentives for investment to make sure the economy does develop sufficient upward momentum. It makes all the more regrettable the Senate filibuster that blocked even the modest stimulus program the Clinton administration had proposed in the spring of 1993.

A LONG-RUN STRATEGY

For the longer run, this analysis points to the importance of developing the foundations on which to build sustained growth. We should have a monetary and budget framework that promotes this growth.

This means keeping money and credit as easy as possible. There is no excuse for allowing overblown fears of inflation in a slack economy or parochial banking or financial interests to keep real interest rates high and credit tight.

We should tax the private sector sufficiently to free the resources that we find desirable for the government to command, but no more than that. This is likely to entail a stable debt/GDP ratio in a growing economy. In such an economy, the public should have sufficient financial wealth, including assets in the form of government debt, to generate enough spending to keep the economy prosperous. And that government debt, growing with the economy, will generally be used to finance public investment, in both physical and human capital, to provide for our future.

We should have a fair tax system that minimizes the distortions and inefficiencies that are introduced by the combination of high marginal rates and inordinate exemptions, deductions, incentives, and loopholes, which shrink the base subject to taxation. We must avoid mindless increases in taxes or cuts in desirable outlays to achieve deficit goals that would only obstruct the achievement of full employment of the nation's resources and economic growth consistent with that full employment and freedom of choice.

The notion of a "production function" is that more and better capital makes labor more productive and that more and better labor makes capital more productive. Merely accumulating labor without additional capital, however, lowers the "marginal product" of labor, as labor becomes redundant. And more capital without an increased supply of labor lowers the marginal product of capital and makes new investment less profitable.[9] This suggests that efforts to stimulate private investment may fail if they do not increase the quality and quantity of labor to work with new capital—or the inputs of new research-based technology and public infrastructure that would add to the productivity of private capital.

If the ranks of well-trained, qualified workers and our knowledge and infrastructure base grow and if aggregate demand and purchasing power also grow, the economy will grow. And private investment will be high and growing too.

---

[9] In technical terms of economic theory, there are diminishing returns to labor and to capital, but more capital input raises the marginal product of labor and more labor input raises the marginal product of capital. Or in mathematical terms, while the partial derivatives of output with respect to its inputs are positive, the second derivatives are negative but the cross-partial derivatives are positive.

In an otherwise perfectly functioning free-market economy, however, these conditions may not be met without a significant role for government. A central theme of my analysis has been that we cannot be sure that adequate aggregate demand will always be forthcoming. Indeed, judging from the historical record of generally less than full employment along with recurring recessions, adequate demand has most often been lacking.

With regard to infrastructure, much of it, by its nature a "public good," available to all once it is provided, must be furnished or at least financed by government. And with regard to trained and qualified labor this is even more true.

In a free, capitalist economy employers cannot own their workers or bind them to their firms. Hence it will not pay employers, on their own, to invest in the education and training of workers who will be free to leave them after they have received their training. This investment is justified, however, for the workers themselves and for society as a whole, since the workers and society as a whole will be receiving the benefits. Hence the major role for government in making education possible, effective, and enjoyed to the optimal amount by all of the population.

And finally, the United States must recognize that, even with our economic power, we hardly dominate the world, nor are we immune to the tribulations around us. We should take maximum advantage of the possibilities for specialization and world trade. We should foster the elimination of the direct trade barriers of tariffs, quotas, and other restrictions on the movement of goods and services. We should also promote monetary policies at home and, as far as we can, in foreign countries that allow exchange rates to settle at free-market levels while allowing maximum employment and output. With free movements of goods, services, and interest and exchange rates, we will have nothing legitimate to fear from trade deficits—or surpluses—or from negative or positive net foreign investment and our presumed "debtor"—or creditor—status in the world.

We should encourage the free exchange of ideas and technology even as we advance our own. The prosperity of other nations will not hurt us. The failure to develop our own human and physical resources will.

We should not be frightened into unwise policies by mismeasures or misunderstandings of the cause, nature, and effects of deficits and debt, governmental and national, or of the nature and cause of movements of money, prices, and interest rates. We should pursue monetary and fiscal policies that bring them to optimum amounts and levels.

These optima, however, are not defined in themselves as "balance," or by any particular number. Rather, they are to be determined by what really counts. That, we know by now, is the economic welfare of our people, a welfare measured in terms of nonmarket as well as market production, of having and sharing equitably all the cake we can now, while providing fully for the bakeries of tomorrow.

Index